The Moral Ecology of Markets

Disagreements about the morality of markets – and about self-interested behavior within markets – run deep. They arise from widely differing perspectives within economics and political philosophy that appear to have nothing in common. In this book, Daniel Finn provides a framework for understanding these conflicting points of view. Recounting the arguments for and against markets and self-interest, he argues that every economy must address four fundamental problems: allocation, distribution, scale, and the quality of relations. In addition, every perspective on the morality of markets addresses explicitly or implicitly the economic, political, and cultural contexts of markets, or what Finn terms "the moral ecology of markets." His book enables a dialogue among the various participants in the debate over justice in markets. In this process, Finn engages with major figures in political philosophy, including John Rawls, Robert Nozick, and Michael Walzer, as well as in economics, notably Milton Friedman, Friedrich Hayek, and James Buchanan.

Daniel K. Finn, an economist and a theologian, has written extensively on the relation of ethics and economics. The author of *Just Trading: On the Economics and Ethics of International Trade* and *Toward a Christian Economic Ethic: Stewardship and Social Power,* he received the Thomas F. Divine Award from the Association for Social Ethics for lifetime achievement in contributions to social economics and the social economy.

The Moral Ecology of Markets

Assessing Claims About Markets and Justice

DANIEL K. FINN

Saint John's University

CAMBRIDGE
UNIVERSITY PRESS

CAMBRIDGE UNIVERSITY PRESS
Cambridge, New York, Melbourne, Madrid, Cape Town, Singapore,
São Paulo, Delhi, Dubai, Tokyo, Mexico City

Cambridge University Press
32 Avenue of the Americas, New York, NY 10013-2473, USA

www.cambridge.org
Information on this title: www.cambridge.org/9780521677998

First published 2006
Reprinted 2010

A catalog record for this publication is available from the British Library.

Library of Congress Cataloging in Publication Data
Finn, Daniel K.
The moral ecology of markets : assessing claims about markets and justice /
Daniel K. Finn.
p. cm.
Includes bibliographical references and index.
ISBN 0-521-86082-2 (hardback) – ISBN 0-521-67799-8 (pbk.)
1. Capitalism – Moral and ethical aspects. 2. Distributive justice. I. Title.
HB501.F495   2006
174'.4 – dc22   200501815

ISBN 978-0-521-86082-6 Hardback
ISBN 978-0-521-67799-8 Paperback

To Jacob and Stephanie

Contents

vii

Acknowledgments

Various parts of this book have benefited greatly from the careful advice of a number of people. I am especially indebted to Joseph Friedrich, Douglas Hicks, and Albino Barrera. I have received helpful feedback from Mark Lutz, Barbara Andolson, and a number of other colleagues who responded to earlier versions of arguments presented at the Association for Social Economics, the Society of Christian Ethics, the Catholic Theological Society of America, the Association for Evolutionary Economics, and the American Academy of Religion. I am also indebted to editors whose own work, and that of their anonymous referees, assisted in improving parts of the argument that have appeared in particular journals: Diane Yeager, John Davis, and Michael Fahey.

I have been the beneficiary of careful manuscript preparation by Judy Shank, Kate Kamakahi, and Maggie Schindler. And I have benefited from the research assistance of students Matt Hendricks and Jeff Holdvogt.

I am grateful for permission to publish parts of previously published articles from the *Review of Social Economy* (Chapter 2), *Theological Studies* and the *Journal of Economics Issues* (Chapters 6 and 7), and the *Annual of the Society of Christian Ethics* (Chapter 5). Permission has also been received from Art Resource to publish the photograph of Giotto's fresco "Injustice" that appears in Chapter 6.

In the end, as usual, I can blame none of the shortcomings of this volume on any of the gracious persons who have assisted me. That responsibility I take myself.

The Moral Ecology of Markets

1

Thinking Ethically About Economic Life

Do the standards of morality apply to economic life? Should they? Can they? How?

The daily news is replete with economic issues, and often where both sides of a debate claim that their policy will best serve ordinary people. Should there be tax cuts aimed to stimulate growth or tax increases to pay for underfunded programs? Should electric utility companies face stiffer limits on polluting emissions from their power plants? Should the United States and the nations of Latin America sign a "free trade" agreement? Should the U.S. Congress stiffen the rules for accounting to prevent further corporate scandals like those at Enron? These and many other issues make up the landscape of contemporary economic ethics. Because these issues entail complex economic questions about what would actually be the effects of alternative policies, it might be helpful to begin with a much simpler example.

Most of us would be aghast at a neighbor's being held up at gunpoint and losing several hundred dollars to a mugger. Whether or not we would personally intervene, we would judge this economic loss as thoroughly unjust. However, if our neighbor were laid off from her job at the local manufacturing plant for several months, few would raise an eyebrow, although there might be sympathy for her hardship.

Defenders of the market system argue that the director of human resources at the plant is simply doing his job when sending out the layoff notices. The company president who made the decision to begin the layoffs was "doing his job" as well. He is responsible to the

company's board of directors, who, in turn, have a fiduciary responsibility to the stockholders. Defenders of the layoffs would argue that
it would be unjust for management *not* to look out for stockholders'
interests. They would add that it makes no sense to eliminate profits
to keep employees working, because without profits, the firm will go
out of business and there will be no jobs at all.

However, critics of this argument point out that in most cases layoffs
occur in the absence of any immediate threat of bankruptcy to the firm.
Is the layoff of several hundred workers justified if the intended effect
is not to avoid bankruptcy but simply to increase the profits paid to
corporate stockholders that year? Are there any moral standards to
which a business firm should adhere when considering layoffs?

There is a small manufacturing firm in Minneapolis, Minnesota –
Reell Precision Manufacturing – that by policy does not lay off its
workers during a downturn in demand but rather reduces the wages
and salaries of company employees, including those of management.
Custodial staff and other workers receiving less than the "target wage"
for the firm (approximately the basic rate for manufacturing workers)
are exempted from such wage reductions. This firm has survived and
even thrived over the years, arguing that employee loyalty more than
makes up for any inefficiencies in the process.[1] Not many firms have
tried this approach, but if it turned out that it could work more broadly,
would there be any moral obligation on the part of boards of directors
and stockholders to move to this model and away from the typical
process of layoffs during a recession?

One dominant response to such proposals is that this is an example
of excessive moralizing that, if institutionalized through law, would
undermine the prosperity of the market system. Even though no one
is seriously proposing a law that forbids layoffs, defenders of "free
markets" regularly oppose proposals to use the power of government
to strengthen the hand of labor within the corporation. They argue
that the economic success of Hong Kong and the other "Asian Tiger"
nations – and the dismal records of economic stagnation in developing
nations with activist governments – stands as testimony to the promise
that "free markets" hold out for the world's poor.

---

[1] See Helen J. Alford, O. P., and Michael J. Naughton, *Managing as if Faith Mattered:
Christian Social Principles in the Modern Organization* (Notre Dame, Ind.: University of
Notre Dame Press, 2001), 135–6 and 146–7.

On the other hand, proponents of additional regulations – such as outlawing the hiring of permanent replacement workers during a strike – point to a long list of social legislation that is now accepted even by the vast majority of conservatives but was originally opposed by the powerful of the day. Unemployment insurance, workers' compensation for injury on the job, anti-discrimination laws, and sexual harassment laws were all opposed by business interests. To take but one example, in the debates about the establishment of Social Security during the Great Depression, Republican Representative James Tabor of New York argued that "never in the history of the world has any measure been brought here so insidiously designed as to prevent business recovery, to enslave workers, and to prevent any possibility of employers providing work for people."[2] Contrary to Tabor's dramatic rhetoric, the economy did recover, businesses went on employing people, and today Social Security is universally recognized as the single greatest reason for lower poverty rates among the elderly. Proponents of such regulations aimed at "humanizing" the market economy remind opponents of the exaggerated claims made by reactionary forces throughout history.[3]

The complexity of these arguments is daunting. There are intricate debates about the empirical impact of various possible government regulations and equally contested arguments about what is morally appropriate. Within the mainstream of the discipline of economics, moral questions are explicitly avoided, out of a conviction that the economist's strength is not in moral but rather in empirical analysis. Economists tend to presume that each economic actor is interested in pursuing only his or her own self-interest. To estimate the effect of a change in, say, a business regulation or tax policy, economists explain that their model reasonably presumes that people will make adjustments in a way that most benefits themselves or most reduces the harm of the necessary change in their own activities.

But critics of this approach in economics object that the picture of economic life taught to tens of thousands of college students in introductory economics courses every year encourages a dispassionate,

---

[2] Arthur J. Altmeyer, *The Formative Years of Social Security* (Madison: University of Wisconsin Press, 1968), 37–8.
[3] Albert O. Hirschman, *The Rhetoric of Reaction: Perversity, Futility, Jeopardy* (Cambridge, Mass.: Harvard University Press, 1992).

amoral orientation toward economic life, one that tacitly presumes efficiency as the goal of economic life while ignoring morality.

Parallel to the influence of economic thinking about the economy is the even more powerful effect of personal experience in a market economy. Critics of "free markets" argue that as both employees and consumers, people quickly learn that if they don't "look out for Number One," no one else will. And this growing concern for getting the most out of economic life slowly undermines traditional ties of communal concern that used to characterize human culture in nearly every part of the Earth.

Economists focus on small, "marginal" changes, investigating the effects caused elsewhere when any one piece of the system changes. But this approach in any discipline tends to ignore the larger institutional framework within which these changes occur and thus often ignores the cumulative change that a long series of marginal changes will cause. Broad cultural shifts can occur, undermining fundamental moral values. Examples of such critiques from the right include William Bennett's assessment of the erosion of education in Western culture.[4] Critiques from the left point to the drop in the economic security of the average worker and in the position of the labor movement more generally even in a culture in which most persons are themselves workers rather than wielders of the power of property ownership.

Daily life is filled with moral valuation. The very choice to make money is a moral one. Ironically, even economists, whose discipline calls for them to avoid moral judgments, exhibit a remarkable degree of moral commitment in their own vocational decision. Most, when asked why they are economists, report that they want to fix problems in the economic system, or improve the lot of the poor, or contribute to the growth of freedom in the world – responses heard from politically conservative as well as from liberal economists.

Perhaps the most frustrating part of conversations about morality and economic life is the cacophony of voices addressing morality in economic life. Left, right, and center seem to be starting from radically different places and consequently often make arguments that

[4] See, for example, William Bennett, *Our Children and Our Country: Improving America's Schools and Affirming the Common Culture* (New York: Simon & Schuster, 1998).

are simply unacceptable from opponents' perspectives. An attitude of the "culture wars" often dominates. Arguments are not made in an attempt to persuade opponents (where one must take seriously the other's point of view in formulating an argument that an opponent will find persuasive) but rather to confirm the convictions of those already faithful to one's own position (where commonly held assumptions can go conveniently unchallenged).

This book proposes a common framework of issues on which all perspectives, from right to left, about the morality of markets already take a position. Although a common framework will not by itself resolve the disputes, it can make possible a conversation, a dialogue, about strengths and weaknesses of market institutions and their moral context.

The book is divided into two parts, with Part I (Chapters 2–5) focusing on the market as a moral issue and Part II (Chapters 6–8) articulating the framework for analyzing both markets and their moral context, here named "the moral ecology of markets."

Chapter 2 reviews the efforts of three well-known economists – Milton Friedman, James Buchanan, and Friedrich Hayek – to defend markets without recourse to moral argument. In each case these efforts fail, in that each scholar requires (and quietly employs) some form of moral commitment beyond self-interest by citizens to sustain even a libertarian view of markets. Arguments about markets inevitably have a moral dimension, and all participants in the debate are better off to admit this at the start.

Chapter 3 reviews the moral defense of markets and outlines a number of moral arguments frequently cited for "free" markets, those that are generally unrestricted by government regulation. Chapter 4 runs in parallel with Chapter 3, outlining the moral critique of self-interest and markets and the various arguments in favor of putting limits on them.

Chapter 5 outlines the four fundamental problems that all economic systems must address: the allocation of scarce resources to alternative uses, the distribution of goods and services to various persons in the economy, the scale of the economy in the biosphere, and the relations that exist among persons in economic life. The chapter investigates each problem and the extent to which efforts to solve one problem affect the others, in some ways making their solutions more difficult and in other ways more feasible.

Part II begins with Chapter 6, outlining a view of markets and beginning with a spatial metaphor: Markets are arenas within which individuals encounter one another to make or respond to economic offers. The arena itself is defined by the fences that form its perimeter, with each fence representing a prohibition of some activity considered abusive. The chapter briefly recounts the views of various perspectives from left to right politically and economically. It finds that, although the list of abusive activities grows as one moves from left to right on the political spectrum, all commentators, including those on the far right, require that there be some government prohibitions of abusive behaviors before they can have any confidence that the voluntary interaction of self-interested individuals in the market can be just.

Chapter 7 completes this perspective of "the moral ecology of markets" by outlining the three other elements that make up any market's moral context. These include the provision of "essential" goods and services, the morality of individuals and groups, and the presence of the institutions of civil society. Although significant disagreements exist about the proper structuring of each of these three elements, all perspectives from right to left explicitly address, or at least implicitly assume, a preferred structure in each area.

The fundamental argument, then, of Chapters 6 and 7 is that there is indeed an ethically respectable "economic defense of self-interest" in markets, but this argument is often misunderstood, especially by those who most frequently make it. The valid form of the argument is that if the four elements of the moral ecology of markets are properly defined and structured, then one can trust that voluntary interaction of individuals within markets will result in just outcomes. Thus, it turns out to be wrong to ask the question "Are markets just?" Markets by themselves cannot be adequately judged to be just or unjust. Rather, for all points of view from left to right, the assessment of justice will depend not only on the structure for markets themselves but also on the context of markets – that is, on the other three elements of the moral ecology of markets.

Chapter 8 concludes with a summary of the argument of the book and with an extension of it to observe that the activity of lobbying governments, particularly by corporations, cannot be defended by means of the economic defense of self-interest. Although arguments exist within political theory to justify such activity, an awareness of the moral ecology of markets leads one to recognize that the economic defense of self-interest is bounded by and exists only within well-defined "rules of the game." Because lobbying is an attempt to change the rules of the game, the economic defense of self-interest cannot be extended to warrant the exertion of self-interest within the governmental process.

The most fundamental argument of this book is that the lack of a true dialogue on the morality of markets cannot be attributed to the depth of disagreement on the issues at stake but must instead be ascribed to a failure of mutual understanding on the part of the contending parties. Admittedly, the debate over markets becomes more complex when we include not only a careful empirical analysis but the necessary moral analysis as well. The difficulty inherent in this necessary process, however, is not an adequate reason for avoiding it altogether.

PART I

SELF-INTEREST, MORALITY, AND THE PROBLEMS OF ECONOMIC LIFE

2

De-Moralized Economic Discourse About Markets

Debates about the proper shape of economic institutions are at least as old as the effort to understand economic life. For most of the past 150 years, this debate has been largely understood as a contest between "capitalism" and "socialism," but it has been characterized more by the force of conviction of the adversaries than by any efforts to understand the opponents' positions.

One classic example of the misrepresentation of the debate over capitalism and socialism has been the treatment of the issue in the vast majority of introductory economics textbooks. Quite typical is the assertion that there are fundamentally two ways to organize an economy: by free markets or by central planning, often with the United States and the former Soviet Union as the classic examples provided. This argument badly misconstrues the real debate between capitalism and socialism, as it ignores the fact that the socialist parties of the industrialized nations of the West have for decades rejected the central planning model dominant in the Soviet Union. The real economic debates in which orthodox economists have been engaged in their home countries have not been with Soviet-style central planners but largely with political forces only somewhat further to the left than they, usually "liberals," "progressives," or democratic socialists.

Not only have introductory economics textbooks misdescribed the debate, but the prevalent political interpretation of the end of the Soviet Union exemplifies the same error. Time and again, commentators on the right have argued that the collapse of Moscow-style central planning is proof that "socialism is dead."[1] Simultaneously, however, the socialists of the industrialized West found that the transformation of Soviet communism caused them no conceptual problems.[2] Nearly all of them had long condemned the Soviets and had argued that the USSR gave socialism a bad name. Politically, of course, things were different. Many ordinary citizens joined the pundits in the belief that socialism was now dead. This has indeed caused problems for Western socialist parties. The point here, however, is that the inadequacy of the earlier debate between capitalism and socialism became even clearer with the demise of the Soviet Union and the transformation of Eastern Europe.

This interpretation of the fall of the Soviet communism is a vivid example of a self-serving overconfidence on the right. Analogous over-simplifications have historically occurred on the left as well. Capitalism has been regularly attacked as a ruthless and unprincipled system oriented solely to the benefit of the capitalist class. Often completely ignored in this analysis is the fact that living standards for most ordinary workers have risen dramatically in capitalist nations over the past two centuries.

Throughout these ideological controversies, each side has tended to excoriate the ideological simplicities and intellectual insularity of their opponents. Each group has conversed almost exclusively with persons of like mind and has regularly launched monologues against what they see as the complete inadequacy of the opposing position. Listeners to this debate have most frequently come to the conclusion that the arguments on the two sides are so different as to be largely incommensurable.

In response, a number of economists have attempted to provide purely scientific arguments in defense of the capitalist system – explicitly eschewing any recourse to a moral framework. Unfortunately, this approach has taken the argument about markets down a path away from the dialogue on both empirical and moral issues that needs to occur.

---

[1] Francis Fukuyama, "The End of History?" *The National Interest* 15 (Summer 1989): 3–18; Robert Heilbroner, "Reflections: The Triumph of Capitalism," *The New Yorker* 64 (January 1989): 98–109.

[2] Michael Lowy, "Twelve Theses on the Crisis of 'Really Existing Socialism,'" *Monthly Review* 43 (May 1991): 33–40; Phillip Eden, John Weeks, and Luken Robinson, "The Triumph of Capitalism? Three Responses," *Monthly Review* 41 (November 1989): 51–8.

We can perhaps best understand the ultimate futility of this attempt to resolve the debate over economic systems without moral argumentation by focusing on the work of Milton Friedman, James Buchanan, and Friedrich Hayek, whom we may take as broadly representative of the Chicago, Public Choice, and Austrian schools of economics, respectively. Of course, none of these three Nobel Prize–winning economists speaks for all the other members of his school of thought, but as the most prominent representatives, these three have been widely influential, both within and beyond their respective groups.

Milton Friedman

Milton Friedman employs three arguments for endorsing capitalism without recourse to a debate over conflicting moral values.

His first argument denies the validity of most moral argumentation surrounding debates over economic policy. Although he counts on broad societal agreement about the immorality of murder, rape, and other crimes of physical force, Friedman tends to view *moral* disagreements on economic issues as fundamental differences about which there can be no rational argumentation and in the midst of which one should not hope for rational progress. Within this view, the moral convictions relative to economic life are akin to a preference for chocolate or vanilla in the choice of ice cream. As he phrases it, "men can ultimately only fight" about fundamental differences in basic values.[3]

Friedman's second argument is that in most cases people have common values but disagree about an empirical question: which policies will best serve those ends. The classic example here is the minimum wage law. He asserts that if those who endorse the minimum wage knew its actual effects on unemployment, they would withdraw their endorsement. Here and in a wide variety of policy issues, Friedman believes that "differences about economic policy among disinterested citizens derived predominantly from different predictions about the economic consequences of taking actions – differences that in principle can be eliminated by the progress of positive economics."[4] In doing this, of course, he ignores the diversity of economic findings

---

[3] Milton Friedman, "The Methodology of Positive Economics," in *Essays in Positive Economics* (Chicago: University of Chicago Press, 1953), 5.
[4] Ibid.

among economists. But the point here is that he makes no attempt to analyze the moral argument, held implicitly by most proponents of the minimum wage, that a prosperous country like the United States should be able to provide a "living wage" to all persons working forty hours a week.[5]

Friedman's argument, of course, is that many defenders of the minimum wage are unaware that it will cause any increase in unemployment among low-wage workers. But the economic shortcomings of many of his adversaries ought not justify Friedman's own inadequate ethical reasoning. The more careful argument for the minimum wage – which he largely ignores – is that there is and must be a moral consensus that acts as the glue which holds society together. In this case, it requires a prosperous nation to guarantee a minimal standard of living to all full-time workers, even if that necessitates a more extensive (and expensive) social safety net for the unemployed. Adequately assessing such arguments requires both economic and ethical sophistication. In his critique of minimum wage legislation, Friedman ignores the moral arguments involved.

The third element of Friedman's position is his belief in the fundamental importance of freedom for humans. He speaks of freedom as the most important value: It is "our ultimate goal in judging social arrangements."[6] A major aim is "to leave the ethical problem for the individual to wrestle with."[7] Because Friedman believes moral values are adjudicated only by an internal process of subjective preference and because no rational progress can be made in interpersonal conversation about values, freedom plays the role of the only feasible value on which to rely in the face of the inevitable conflicts among people in democratic societies. In a sense, Friedman has taken the classic liberal virtue of tolerance into the public realm and has generalized it into the single moral value that trumps all others, that one moral value which is to structure all of human society.

Friedman presumes that his readers agree with him that the evils of physical force and fraud should be eliminated by law – and that

---

5 Robert E. Prasch and Falguni Sheth, "The Economics and Ethics of Minimum Wage Legislation," *Review of Social Economy* 57 (1999): 466–87.

6 Milton Friedman, *Capitalism and Freedom* (Chicago: University of Chicago Press, 1962), 12.

7 Ibid.

society should invest the resources necessary to do so – but he makes
no comprehensive intellectual defense of this moral conviction. Just
as important, he offers few arguments for why government should
expend resources to defend the values at stake in force and fraud but
not other values in other contexts, such as health care, or education,
or basic food and shelter for those who are unable to provide them for
themselves. He instead spends more time articulating the inefficiencies that such additional government activities would entail. He makes
an empirical claim against the moral arguments of his opponents in
such a way, he hopes, that the line between acceptable and unacceptable government behavior does not need to be defended morally.

Friedman goes even further to assert that "underlying most arguments against the free market is a lack of belief in freedom itself."[8] In
this he seems to forget that his own endorsement of governmental prohibition of force and fraud differs only in degree, not in kind, from the
position of others who would prohibit a longer list of perceived abuses
than he. Even Friedman would oppose "completely" free markets, as
the absence of all restrictions on behavior would mean allowing murder as a legal tactic in economic competition. As we shall see in Chapter 7, concerning the moral ecology of markets, such presumptions do
indeed require a moral argument, and Friedman's own approach to
these simply keeps that argument implicit and, unfortunately, under-
developed.

James Buchanan

Milton Friedman is willing to venture back and forth from economic
analysis to political philosophy without much apparent worry about
the methodological difficulties involved. James Buchanan quite explicitly takes up the evaluation of markets from a scientific point of
view. His method is "profoundly individualistic, in an ontological-
methodological sense ... and the methodological individualist is necessarily precluded from the projection of his own values."[9] Buchanan

---

[8] Ibid., 15.

[9] Buchanan goes on to say that "his role must remain more circumscribed than that of
the collectivist-cum-elitist who is required to specify objectives for social action that
are independent from individual values other than his own and those of his cohorts."

describes his own work, so fundamental to the whole field of "public choice economics," as an attempt to employ the usual presumptions of economic science to investigate group decision making, and in particular, decisions by government and about the creation of a constitutional democracy "conducted by free individuals attempting to formulate generally acceptable rules in their own long-term interest."[10] Buchanan wants to further the public interest,[11] but he does not provide a defense for this obviously normative goal.

The question we are interested in posing about any particular social order is whether the rules by which individual actions are coordinated are such as to transform actions undertaken by participants in their own private interests into outcomes that are in the interest of others. We know that this curious alchemy is in fact worked by the market – that the invisible hand operates, under certain more or less well defined conditions, to convert private interest into public interest.[12]

The political philosopher Joseph Cropsey has described Adam Smith's invisible hand as "an ancient simplicity [that] man's integration in the order of nature is beneficial rather than threatening to humanity, and is concordant with man's sociality and his virtue."[13] Buchanan's confidence here, unlike Smith's, is less rooted in nature than in the characteristics of human interaction. Nonetheless, like Smith, he remains convinced that "public interest is served by the market order. No such demonstration can be made with respect to alternative arrangements."[14]

James M. Buchanan, *The Limits of Liberty: Between Anarchy and Leviathan* (Chicago: University of Chicago Press, 1975), 1.

[10] James M. Buchanan and Gordon Tullock, *The Calculus of Consent: Logical Foundations of Constitutional Democracy* (Ann Arbor: University of Michigan Press, 1962), 7.

[11] For Buchanan, "the only purpose of science is its ultimate assistance in the development of normative propositions. We seek to learn how the world works in order to make it work 'better,' and to 'improve things': this is as true for physical science as it is for social science." Buchanan and Tullock, *Calculus of Consent*, 308.

[12] Geoffrey Brennan and James M. Buchanan, "The Normative Purpose of Economic 'Science': Rediscovery of an Eighteenth Century Method," in James M. Buchanan and Robert D. Tollison, eds., *The Theory of Public Choice II* (Ann Arbor: University of Michigan Press, 1984), 388.

[13] Joseph Cropsey, *Polity and Economy: With Further Thoughts on the Principles of Adam Smith* (South Bend, Ind.: Saint Augustine's Press, 2001), 166.

[14] Brennan and Buchanan, "Normative Purpose," 392.

Like Friedman, Buchanan himself wants to provide a nonmoral defense of freedom. His analysis attempts to find "better" institutional structures, but he wishes to defend the judgment in an amoral way. Improving individual behavior is a moral matter, he says, but "problems of social organization need not be moral problems."[15]

A situation is judged "good" to the extent that it allows individuals to get what they want to get, whatsoever this might be, limited only by the principle of mutual agreement. Individual freedom becomes the overriding objective for social policy, not as an instrumental element in attaining economic or cultural bliss, and not as some metaphysically superior value, but much more simply as a necessary consequence of an individualist-democratic methodology.[16]

Although professionals in ethics would insist that this definition of a "good" situation is indeed based on a moral judgment, Buchanan understands this stress on individual liberty as arising not from any subjective valuation on his part but from the methodology of individualism.

He begins by presuming that individuals are self-interested, in the sense that they will seek their own goals. He occasionally notes that this does not mean that all persons are "selfish," but he more often asserts that in most decisions most people will have their own interests primarily in mind.[17]

In a strictly personalized sense, any person's ideal situation is one that allows him full freedom of action and inhibits the behavior of others so as to force adherence to his own desires. That is to say, each person seeks mastery over a world of slaves.[18]

Although he does not say much about it, Buchanan sees this presumption of self-interest as a sort of "weak assumption," one that will not demand a leap of faith by his readers.[19] Here he takes himself to

---

[15] Buchanan and Tullock, *Calculus of Consent*, 310.
[16] Buchanan, *Limits of Liberty*, 2.
[17] The theory of public choice posits that "the theory of markets postulates only that the relationship be *economic*, that the interest of his opposite number in the exchange be excluded from consideration." Buchanan and Tullock, *Calculus of Consent*, 17–18.
[18] Buchanan, *Limits of Liberty*, 92.
[19] This procedure is somewhat similar to that taken by John Rawls in his classic treatise *A Theory of Justice*. Rawls constructs his "original position" with the help of a "weak assumption," that all persons will look out for their own interests (though in the original position they will not know their narrow interests as they are hidden from

be developing a more realistic model of political behavior than traditional political philosophy has provided, where political leaders have
too often been presumed to have the public good in mind when they
enter the political realm.[20] A central element in public choice theory
is the presumption that leaders, whether in neighborhood groups or
in national parliaments, exhibit the same behavior in decision making
as do all other persons. That is, people seek their own interests; and for
political leaders, the primary interest is staying in office. Thus, elected
officials will tend to endorse and vote for those positions that are most
likely to get them reelected.

Buchanan presents only anecdotal evidence in favor of this model
of self-interest for both the common citizen and elected office holders.
He simply employs the standard economic model to see what insights
it might provide. It is quite clear, however, that in an era when partisans
from both the left and the right provide a strong critique of the narrow
interests so often served within the political process, many readers
may be inclined to suppose the empirical adequacy of this *a priori*
assumption.

The model Buchanan develops addresses both constitutional and
legislative questions and comes to the general conclusion that in a
modern democracy there is an inevitable tendency for governments
to raise taxes ever higher to pay out ever greater benefits to influential
interest groups because of the fundamental dynamics of the majority
vote system. Politicians can ensure that they'll stay in office if they
maintain the support of at least 51 percent of their voting constituents.
As "political entrepreneurs," office holders try to promise benefits to
enough different interest groups to garner support from a sufficiently
large coalition. Because the self-interest of each group in the coalition

any specific knowledge about their genetic assets or their place in the social system).
See John Rawls, *Theory of Justice* (Cambridge, Mass.: Harvard University Press, 1971),
18. Buchanan himself proposes a "less normative" starting point than Rawls', in that he
attempts to explain how rights and rules for behavior "emerge from the nonidealistic,
self-interested behavior of men, without any presumption of equality in some original
position – equality either actually or expectationally." Buchanan, *Limits of Liberty*, 54.

[20] As Buchanan and Tullock have sarcastically put it, for most political theorists, "the
choice-making process has been conceived of as the means of arriving at some version
of 'truth,' some rationalist absolute which remains to be discovered through reason
or revelation, in which, once discovered, will attract all men to its support." Buchanan
and Tullock, *Calculus of Consent*, 4.

almost always comes at the expense of others, politicians stay in office
by taxing the whole citizenry and redirecting the benefits to the groups
whose support is needed if they are to stay in office.

Buchanan does not approve of this process, but he makes no moral
argument that legislators should have – or that citizens should press
them to develop – a higher moral sense that would put the greater
good of the community ahead of their own personal interests. Rather,
he articulates the alternative strategies that might arise from the self-
interested decisions of citizens to subvert the pork barrel politics that
the model predicts.

Buchanan's fundamental policy proposal is that the authority of leg-
islatures must be severely curtailed so that they are not free to spend
the money needed to sustain this tax-and-spend system. He recom-
mends a political strategy that would be termed "conservative" in the
United States, as it would recommend a significant reduction in the
activities of government – because he sees such a plan as the only
realistic means for limiting this modern-day version of a democratic
leviathan. He calls for a formal constitutional convention, within which
self-interested citizens would limit what their legislature can do by with-
drawing the constitutional authority to raise taxes continually in order
to pay out ever more benefits to form a majority coalition.

Most interesting for our purposes here is the fact that even
Buchanan's constitutional convention would require political decisions by representatives of the people charged with reforming a constitution. Of course, following the logic of public choice theory, it would
seem that no individual citizen committed to Buchanan's vision of a
good constitution would have sufficient incentive to become involved
in the pre–constitutional reform process simply out of self-interest.
Because any individual's expected impact on the process is so small,
the loss of time and resources would outweigh any expected gain.
Thus, those involved in the political process to reconstruct the constitution would seem to be either political entrepreneurs (who, just as
in ordinary government, would be attempting to assemble a majority
coalition to take over the constitutional convention for self-interested
gain) or persons with some sort of higher commitment to the common
good (who would be willing to expend more energy and resources than
Buchanan's own model of human behavior would predict). Buchanan
clearly wants the latter group to prevail. More important, he needs

this outcome if he is to sustain any hope of reform of our current democratic system.

Buchanan renders this prospect – a thoroughly unlikely one from the point of view of public choice analysis – more believable in two ways. The first is the conviction of the classical liberal tradition that in the long run there is a harmony of interests – and that people can come to understand which political and economic interests best serve the interests of all. The second is his treatment of the "artifactual" dimensions of human life. By this he means the capacity of humans to choose to change themselves into someone different.[21] Buchanan muses that "perhaps the nonteleological elements of individual choice have been too much neglected by us all."[22] That is, the attempt to interpret all human action as oriented toward preexisting ends of the actor overlooks the fact that, as his mentor Frank Knight put it, "Insofar as a man is wise or good, his 'character' is acquired chiefly by posing as better than he is, until a part of his pretense becomes a habit."[23]

The bulk of Buchanan's work concerns the ordinary political and economic decisions of life – the postconstitutional phase – and incorporates the traditional economic presumption of self-interest. His treatment of preconstitutional decisions relies on a quite different "constitutional attitude,"[24] because of which the individual engages in "changing the basic rules of social order in the direction of imagined good societies."[25] Buchanan does not explicitly identify this process as requiring a less self-interested set of values. He instead appeals to "the elementary fact that the selection of the rules, 'constitutional choice,' is of a different attitudinal dimension from the selection of strategies within defined rules."[26] It does not seem unfair to note that "a different attitudinal dimension" is a public choice euphemism for a less selfish moral attitude that values some version of a "common good" above one's own self-interest.

---

[21] James M. Buchanan, "Natural and Artifactual Man," in *What Should Economists Do?* (Indianapolis: Liberty Press, 1979), Chapter 5.

[22] Ibid., 109.

[23] Frank Knight, "The Planful Act: The Possibilities & Limitations of Collective Rationality," in *Freedom & Reform* (New York: Harper & Brothers, 1947), 104. Cited in James M. Buchanan, "Natural & Artifactual Man."

[24] Buchanan, "Natural & Artifactual Man," 106.

[25] Ibid., 110.

[26] Ibid., 107.

This anomaly in Buchanan's work – starting from a model's presumption of self-interest and yet needing to have a fundamental concern for the common good at a constitutional convention – exhibits in another way the futility of economists' amoral defense of markets. Whether at the level of the constitution or the legislature, somewhere at some point people need to put a sense of the common good ahead of their own selfish interests, or some majority will have the power (and claim the moral right) to design a system to their own partisan benefit. Buchanan's own hope seems to be that the scientific insight provided through public choice theory will encourage more people to undergo "the libertarian shift."[27]

We should also note that Buchanan's move from a descriptive economic model to normative conclusions about real constitutional and legislative life is a pervasive methodological error among contemporary mainstream economists. A century and a half ago, John Stuart Mill presumed economists should study individuals as trying to maximize their wealth. Mill, however, recognized that this was not the only motive in life.[28] For this reason when public policy questions were to be resolved, the findings of economics were relevant but Mill admitted that they had to be employed alongside the findings of all the other relevant social and natural sciences. The policy makers then applied an overall moral framework before reliable policy propositions could be generated. Buchanan typically exhibits a kind of moral agnosticism, as would be appropriate with his economic model, but he also presses for practical (i.e., normative) conclusions for public policy. Such conclusions are methodologically unfounded – because his starting point is simply a particular model chosen arbitrarily, with no claim to empirical accuracy. Buchanan's ventures into the realm of moral pronouncements about good or bad public policy are more subtle than Friedman's, but without a moral argument to undergird them, they are similarly unwarranted.

One important issue that exemplifies Buchanan's approach is his beginning with the status quo in society. In a reaction against traditional political philosophy that begins with an idealized goal toward

---

[27] Buchanan, *Limits of Liberty*, 128.
[28] John Stuart Mill, *Essays on Some Unsettled Questions of Political Economy* (London: Longmans, Green, Reader and Dyer, 1874), 138.

which society should move, Buchanan prefers to begin with the current situation in society and asks what societal improvements can be made through the voluntary agreement of citizens. Buchanan's commitment to a libertarian perspective finds economic expression in his requirement that any such changes respect the criterion of Pareto efficiency. Expressed politically, this requires that there be unanimous consent for any change.

Warren Samuels, in a public exchange of correspondence with Buchanan, has challenged Buchanan's presumption that this approach is simply descriptive and not normative. As Buchanan expressed it, "I am not taking an advocacy position grounded on my own or anyone else's values."[29] Samuels presents several telling objections to this perspective, two of which are most helpful here.

The first is that although Buchanan would require that all governmental change respect the unanimity-of-consent rule, there are numerous changes in the market that are not Pareto-optimal in this same sense but Buchanan approves of them nonetheless. Two economic actors in the market often come to an economic agreement that makes others – at times even a large majority of the population – worse off. Yet Buchanan's approach means that the majority has no right to limit such activities, because these two individuals (like every individual) have veto power in government through the unanimous-consent rule.

Second, and more telling, every *existing* legal and economic institution was originally the result of a decision process in which the unanimity-of-consent rule did not apply, resulting in a world shaped in the interests of the most powerful of that bygone day. As Samuels put it, to now require unanimity before any political change can occur "allows the privileged in the status quo to hold out and perpetuate themselves by being able to withhold their consent.... It places too much power in the hands of already privileged, indeed cementing their mortgage upon the future."[30]

---

[29] James M. Buchanan and Warren Samuels, "On Some Fundamental Issues in Political Economy: An Exchange of Correspondence," *Journal of Economic Issues* 9 (March 1975): 24.

[30] Ibid., 30.

There is an implicit normative choice on Buchanan's part in his methodological decision to privilege the status quo, and at one point Buchanan reluctantly concedes that it is a "value judgment."[31] Unfortunately, in his subsequent scholarly work Buchanan seems to forget this admission. In fact, his reluctant privileging of the status quo (he tells Samuels, "I do not especially like the status quo defense my methodology forces me into, but where can I go?") seems itself to arise from a conviction that rational progress on values through dialogue is ultimately impossible.[32]

On a few occasions, Buchanan shows an explicit interest in furthering the morality of persons in society. In an essay entitled "We Should All Pay the Preacher," he argues that "if the institutions of moral-ethical persuasion, which I have called 'the preacher' in the title for this chapter, are even marginally effective, each party to a potential interaction will have some incentive to 'pay the preacher'...."[33] In this context Buchanan makes a remarkable admission concerning the inadequacy of an economics separated from ethics. In the end he believes that "we should all pay the right preacher," a normative presumption rather surprising in a positive analysis. "For all practical purposes, public or social capital may be permanently lost once it is destroyed. It may be impossible to secure its replacement, at least on the basis of rational decisions made by individuals."[34] Furthermore, economists are to blame: "The absence of such understanding must be laid squarely on the shoulders of the economists, who have separated economics from its initial moorings as part of moral philosophy."[35] He concludes with a call for economists "to bring their science back into its proper relationship to ethics."[36] By this call, Buchanan acknowledges

---

[31] Ibid., 33.

[32] Ibid., 19.

[33] Buchanan adds that there will be the tendency of "free-ridership" in that, for any individual, withholding financial support for the preacher will have little effect on how many preachers are active in a large society. He does not tell us why this free-rider problem would not predominate, leading to the disappearance of preachers for lack of payments. James M. Buchanan, *Ethics and Economic Progress* (Norman: University of Oklahoma Press, 1994), 70.

[34] Buchanan, *Limits of Liberty*, 126.

[35] Buchanan, *Ethics and Economic Process*, 82.

[36] Ibid., 83.

the importance of personal morality, but he inexplicably does not integrate this insight into his own amoral analysis of economic and political systems.

Buchanan's ultimate concern about morality may seem to be a minor personal interest, but systematically it is related to his awareness that the smooth operation of the "ordered anarchy" to which he looks forward requires "the set of manners, the customary modes for personal behavior, which reflect the mutual acceptance of limits."[37] While law prevents the worst violations here, Buchanan recognizes that in every culture many people spontaneously respect limits even when they might not have to. In fact, Buchanan laments the eroding of "traditional codes of conduct," a problem he attributes to the counterculture of the 1960s. What he refers to as custom and manner are, from a more robust point of view, often described by others as shared values and social meanings within a culture. This moral ethos of a culture is almost completely ignored by Buchanan within his model even though it is quite clear that he depends upon it for the ordinary operation of daily life within his ordered anarchy. In this way, as in other ways we have seen, Buchanan in the end needs a (missing) moral argument for the structure of thought he erects.

Friedrich Hayek

Friedrich Hayek represents our third example of an attempt to defend markets by means of a largely amoral analysis. A generation before both Friedman and Buchanan, Hayek, more than any other single person, might be credited with the revival of that passionate commitment to freedom in economic and political affairs that has more recently been termed "libertarianism." At the end of World War II, after the spending of the war had brought both the Great Depression to a definitive end and Keynesian fiscal policy to mainstream supremacy, Friedrich Hayek brought together a small group of conservative intellectuals to form the Mont Pèlerin Society. Hayek's own work, extending for nearly another half-century, remains as one of the most articulate defenses of the broadly libertarian political agenda that both Friedman

---

[37] Buchanan, *Limits of Liberty*, 20.

and Buchanan, employing quite different analyses, also endorse. He attempts – at times explicitly – to argue for the market without recourse to moral warrant. As he puts it in the Introduction to his three-volume work, *Law, Liberty & Legislation*, near the end of his career as a scholar,

The demonstration that the differences between socialists and non-socialists ultimately rests on purely intellectual issues capable of a scientific resolution and not on different judgments of value appears to me one of the most important outcomes of the train of thought pursued in this book.[38]

Hayek does not wish to engage the question of whether humans ought to be guided by a concern for others. He finds this question undercut by an epistemological insight into the limitations of human knowledge.

The real question, therefore, is not whether man is, or ought to be, guided by selfish motives but whether we can allow him to be guided in his actions by those immediate consequences which he can know and care for or whether he ought to be made to do what seems appropriate to somebody else who is supposed to possess a fuller comprehension of the significance of these actions to society as a whole.[39]

Because only the local, individual economic actor can know the particular immediate setting and consequences of decisions, only that actor should have authority over them. This attempt to side-step the question of the moral status of self-interest by an empirical appeal to ignorance conveniently eclipses the fact that Hayek's own ignorance doesn't prevent him from turning to government to ban the use of physical violence against another person – where the immediate consequences are also better known to the perpetrator than to the government.

Elsewhere, Hayek, following a long tradition dating back at least to Bernard Mandeville, is clearly convinced that allowing people to further their own interests redounds to the benefit of others. This might lead us to acknowledge that, in addition to the amoral defense of self-interest based on ignorance just cited, Hayek presents a

---

[38] Friedrich A. Hayek, *Law, Legislation and Liberty*, vol. 1, *Rules and Order* (Chicago: University of Chicago Press, 1973), 6.

[39] Friedrich A. Hayek, *Individualism and Economic Order* (Chicago: University of Chicago Press, 1948), 14.

consequentialist – and perhaps even an "indirect" utilitarian[40] – moral defense as well, because of the superior productivity of a market system based on individual choice. However, it is significant that each time he explicitly treats the issue of self-interest, he alludes only to the argument from ignorance. Although Hayek seems not to have addressed this peculiarity, it is informative to note the treatment of an analogous issue in the work of a much younger libertarian voice, Robert Nozick.

Nozick argues that productivity (of the system of markets and private ownership) is what warrants John Locke's belief that the law of nature is not violated even though there is no longer in Locke's day "enough and as good left in the commons" for others.[41] Yet in spite of Nozick's conviction about the general beneficence of such a market system, he explicitly excludes this consequentialist rationale based in the value of productivity from his argument for a minimal state.[42] The problem, he notes, is that endorsing this element of consequentialism would open the door for opponents to employ similar consequentialist arguments for other forms of governmental restriction of individual freedom if it might be argued that a particular restriction would do more good than harm. Nozick doesn't want to play this consequentialist game, and he says so.

Returning to Hayek, we might guess that the same sorts of concerns lie behind his apparent aversion to addressing such consequentialist arguments about general prosperity when he explicitly defends self-interested action solely on epistemological grounds. This aversion is all the more striking in light of Hayek's willingness to analyze constitutional political structures from a consequentialist perspective.

Where Buchanan argues for a fully rational analysis and improvement of political structures, Hayek is openly disdainful of such rationalist arrogance, though his disdain is directed against opponents on the left and never against his libertarian allies who commit the same sin. He claims, to the contrary, that attempts to construct a better

[40] Chandran Kukathas, *Hayek and Modern Liberalism* (New York: Oxford University Press, 1990), 192–201.
[41] This "Lockean Proviso," as Nozick phrases it, is roughly equivalent to "not leaving others worse off." The greater general prosperity effected by private ownership (and the attendant incentive to invest resources to improve productivity) meets that standard, according to Nozick. *Anarchy, State and Utopia* (Oxford: Blackwell, 1974), 178.
[42] Robert Nozick, *Anarchy*, 177.

political system have always failed and have instead fueled the growth of government.

But the desire to use our reason to turn the whole of society into one rationally directed engine persists, and in order to realize it common ends are imposed upon all that cannot be justified by reason and cannot be more than the decisions of particular wills.[43]

Central to Hayek's analysis here is the notion of a "complex order" formed by a spontaneous process, an interaction of individuals over a long period of time in which the process itself improves spontaneously, without any comprehensive design by the people involved. He quotes Adam Ferguson approvingly in this regard: "Nations stumble upon establishments, which are indeed the result of human action but not the result of human design."[44] As Hayek himself puts it, "The rules which made the growth of this complex order possible were initially not designed in expectation of that result; but those people who happened to adopt suitable rules developed a complex civilization which then often spread to others."[45]

"Nobody can know *who* knows best," so "people are and ought to be guided in *their* actions by their interests and desires . . . they ought to be allowed to strive for whatever *they* think desirable."[46]

Hayek's view of moral values is similar to Friedman's. Particular ends are ultimately "nonrational," and, concerning particular ends, "no rational argument can produce agreement if it is not already present at the outset."[47] This fundamental conviction is what presses Hayek to formulate an amoral defense of the market system. Still, this amoral and social scientific analysis of a spontaneous order requires the social scientist "to accept the values which are indispensable for its existence" – that is, "values on which the whole order rests." Because the spontaneous order of the market and limited democratic government have produced immense advancement in the freedom and prosperity of ordinary people, Hayek is convinced that the goal must be to preserve and extend this order. Thus those largely libertarian moral

[43] Hayek, *Law*, 1:32.
[44] Hayek, *Individualism*, 7.
[45] Hayek, *Law*, 1:50.
[46] Hayek, *Individualism*, 15.
[47] Hayek, *Law*, 1:34.

values necessary for its existence have a sort of scientific endorsement – without, he hopes, any need for a moral argument to ground them.

Hayek is quite interested in justice as "rules of just conduct" for individuals that "serve the formation of a spontaneous order."[48] That is, he views justice as an attribute of individual behavior only, not of institutions like the market or the government. In addition to individualizing the notion of justice, Hayek reduces justice to a matter of "knowledge of the relative importance of the different effects" of an action. He argues that if all persons had complete knowledge "there would be no room for a conception of justice . . . Justice is an adaptation to our ignorance."[49] Similar to Friedman, Hayek here makes no reference to moral judgments necessary in determining what is just but instead insists that it is a matter of knowledge – a further indication of Hayek's attempt to construct an amoral defense of capitalism.

For Hayek, the results of a spontaneous order can neither be just nor unjust, because no single rational agent is bringing them about. If a process is "not subject to human control," it is not and cannot be either just or unjust.[50] It is likely that even if every participant in the market were to follow the rules of justice, in the end some individual or group would suffer a setback or misfortune and would conclude that injustice had occurred. For Hayek, this conclusion is wrongheaded because

there is no individual and no cooperating group of people against which the sufferer would have a just complaint and there are no conceivable rules of just individual conduct which would at the same time secure a functioning order and prevent such disappointments.[51]

All attempts to assess the justice of a spontaneous order are based on an intellectual mistake. In fact, Hayek is more disdainful of the notion of "social justice" than of any other idea he criticizes.

The term is intellectually disreputable, the mark of demagogy or cheap journalism which responsible thinkers ought to be ashamed to use because, once its vacuity is recognized, its use is dishonest.[52]

[48] Friedrich A. Hayek, *Law, Legislation and Liberty*, vol. 2, *The Mirage of Social Justice* (Chicago: University of Chicago Press, 1976), 31.
[49] Ibid., 39.
[50] Ibid., 32.
[51] Ibid., 69.
[52] Ibid.

He scorns those who would ask not only if individual market participants have acted justly but also whether markets are just.

Hayek's epistemological conviction about the limits of knowledge – and an appreciation of the kind and quantity of knowledge that only the individual economic actor has – was a central part of his contribution to the "socialist calculation" debate of the 1930s and beyond. Begun by Ludwig von Mises, the debate focused on whether a socialist, centrally planned economic system could, even "in theory," decide on the right (i.e., efficient) prices and quantities for goods and services.[53] In a now classic argument, Hayek asserted that prices in a market system based on private ownership communicate essential information to individual decision makers, who alone have both the information necessary to make efficient decisions and the incentive to do so. Central planners, even if virtuous enough to have the desire, could never have the needed information. Many historians of economic thought have judged the debate a standoff because of theoretical refinements by socialists in response to von Mises' charge. More recently, Austrian economists have argued that the basic insights of von Mises and Hayek about the absence of equilibrium in the real world have yet to be appreciated.[54]

The debate *about* the socialist calculation debate is complicated, but for our purposes it is sufficient to note that it represents a true exception to the general pattern criticized in this chapter. In most of his work, Hayek attempts an amoral defense of the market that actually relies on an unexamined moral position.[55] In the socialist calculation debate, however, he makes a more adequate amoral defense of markets, one that is strengthened considerably by later Austrian refinements of knowledge and agency problems.[56] We should note, of course, that the socialist calculation debate focuses on the

---

[53] Ludwig von Mises, "Economic Calculation in the Socialist Commonwealth," in Friedrich Hayek, ed., *Collectivist Economic Planning: Critical Studies on the Possibilities of Socialism* (London: Routledge, 1935), 87–130.

[54] Don Lavoie, *Rivalry & Central Planning: The Socialist Calculation Debate Reconsidered* (Cambridge: Cambridge University Press, 1985).

[55] Hayek's advocacy of the superiority of markets over central planning includes some "weak" moral assumptions (e.g., preferring a more efficient to a less efficient means to one's goals), but this is true of all practical thought. The focus of this chapter is on more controversial moral commitments.

[56] See Lavoie, *Rivalry*.

difference between markets and central planning. It is much less applicable to debates *within* market systems, something we shall address in Chapters 7 and 8.

Hayek describes the market as a complex order structured by a spontaneous process. He examines the character of complex orders through the example of English common law, in which judges over many centuries employed historical precedents and made decisions to resolve conflicts, with "the aim of improving a given order of actions by laying down a rule that would prevent the reoccurrence of such conflicts as have occurred."[57] Judges faced new problems and brought about slight alterations in the law's treatment of new issues or circumstances, leaving the law at the end of each era better able to resolve problems than at the beginning. Hayek believes that there is an unplanned wisdom in the development of many such institutional structures and that conscious tinkering with them can only make things worse.

Although a liberal (in the nineteenth-century sense), Hayek criticizes "continental" liberalism (and tacitly Buchanan) for the illusion that humans can adequately *decide* the shape of their institutions.[58] He argues that this is a grave mistake: The spontaneous historical development of institutions of greater freedom should be respected and not thwarted out of some false sense that a more just society might be designed to improve on this spontaneous process.[59] As Hayek puts it,

> The fact is, rather, that we can preserve an order of such complexity not by the method of directing the members, but only indirectly by enforcing and improving the rules conducive to the formation of a spontaneous order.[60]

This strong critique of "constructivism" by those on the left who would rationally redesign markets and even constitutions is significantly

---

[57] Hayek, *Law*, 1:101.
[58] Hayek, *Law*, 1:8–34.
[59] Buchanan sees things quite differently: "History need not be a random walk in sociopolitical space, and I have no faith in the efficacy of social evolutionary process. The institutions that survive and prosper need not be those that maximize man's potential. Evolution may produce social dilemma as readily as social paradise." Buchanan, *Limits of Liberty*, 167. For Buchanan's reaction to Hayek, see *Limits of Liberty*, 194, footnote 1.
[60] Hayek, *Law*, 1:51.

weakened by Hayek's willingness to offer his own proposals for improved constitutional design.[61] Although supporters may be willing to look more kindly on the problem, Bruce Caldwell has observed that Hayek's proposals for constitutional reformation stand "in apparent violation of his strictures concerning constructivism."[62] Chandran Kukathas has identified this inconsistency as one of a number of intellectual incoherences within Hayek's thought.[63] Hayek's own understanding of this internal inconsistency is left even more mysterious when, near the end of his life, he spoke warmly of the work of John Rawls, whom most political philosophers would identify with the constructivist wing of modern liberalism.[64]

Both Hayek's aversion to social justice and his belief that spontaneous orders such as the market are endangered by efforts to make them more just play important roles in his amoral defense of capitalism. He inexplicably forgets about two centuries of efforts by a multitude of great economists, legislators, and others to improve markets and instead stresses the futility of morally motivated changes in markets today. Nonetheless, even Hayek would judge as unjust an economic and political system in which certain prevalent crimes of violence went unpunished because of a government decision to allow them. In general, his caution against applying moral argument to improve legal structures rests on a prior and silent moral assessment that the current (spontaneously generated) system already incorporates all necessary legal limitations, and the morally needed change is to increase personal liberty.

Hayek shares with Buchanan and Friedman the conviction that modern democratic governments tax and spend excessively because of the predictable incentives of politicians trying to be reelected. His solution is a bicameral legislature in which the difference between the houses of the legislative branch is not in the form of representation but in the powers granted to each. The upper house would make all

---

[61] Viktor Vanberg, *Rules and Choice in Economics* (London: Routledge, 1994), chaps. 5–7 & 12.
[62] Bruce Caldwell, "Hayek and Socialism," *Journal of Economic Literature* 25 (December 1997): 1873.
[63] Kukathas, *Hayek*, 46–83.
[64] Hayek, *Law*, 2: xiii; Kukathas, *Hayek*, 209.

the laws, the "rules of just conduct,"[65] and would be responsible for legal justice in society. An additional duty of the upper house of the legislature would be to define the authority and budget of the lower house. The lower house would make concrete decisions concerning government expenditures, but because their authority was already limited by the decisions of the upper house, they could not resort to the excesses of taxing and spending to which an unrestricted legislature would inevitably succumb.

And yet when it comes to the question of who should be elected to the upper house, Hayek faces the same quandary that Buchanan does in his constitutional convention. He has to hope that those persons elected to this supreme legislative body will not act out of a narrow self-interest that might lead them to define the legal structures for their own benefit at the expense of others. He argues that citizens will be electing "persons whom they can trust to uphold justice impartially" and will choose those with "probity, wisdom, judgment."[66] Hayek acknowledges that citizens electing representatives to the lower house, where particular interests are adjudicated, would not look for such general virtues, but he thinks that because the powers of the upper house are more restricted, citizens might "be induced to respond by designating those whose judgment they have learned most to respect."[67] He does not have within his system the grounds for arguing that people *ought* to have this public-spiritedness rather than act to further their own interests, but he needs them to do so here. Like Buchanan's, his system requires a moral attitude in favor of some form of common good. This in turn requires a moral argument, one that his amoral endorsement of markets cannot provide.

[65] Friedrich A. Hayek, *Law, Legislation and Liberty*, vol. 3, *The Political Order of a Free People* (Chicago: University of Chicago Press, 1979), 119.

[66] Ibid., 112.

[67] To encourage such public-spiritedness, Hayek calls for these legislators in the upper assembly to serve for fifteen years and to be elected only after "they have already have proved themselves in the ordinary business of life." He proposes that "each group of people of the same age once in their lives, say in the calendar year in which they reach the age of 45, [would] select from their midst representatives to serve for fifteen years." Ibid., 113. It is ironic that the age of 45 was also used as the first year citizens were allowed to vote for president in the 1888 socialist utopian novel, *Looking Backward*. Edward Bellamy, *Looking Back* (New York: New American Library, 1960), 132.

Conclusion

In sum, the attempts by Friedman, Buchanan, and Hayek to defend markets without recourse to moral arguments are unsuccessful. Each of these economists is aware of the complexity of the moral debate about markets. In hopes of resolving the debate without having to address these complications, they have proposed analyses of the market that have eschewed or explicitly disparaged any moral assessment of the market system. Ultimately, however, each needs a strong moral stance to complete his own vision, and these moral positions cannot themselves be defended on the amoral grounds they propose. Of the three, Buchanan's work demonstrates the greatest awareness of the moral inadequacy of the amoral endorsement of self-interest in markets. However, the awareness does not in the end lead him to alter his fundamental approach to the issue.

An adequate analysis of markets, whether a defense or a critique, must include an articulation of their moral underpinnings, including the moral significance of the other institutional elements that form the context for markets. We will return to these issues in Chapters 7 and 8, but first we must address that issue of central importance in any moral assessment of economic life: self-interest.

3

The Moral Defense of Self-Interest and Markets

"That was our plan. It was based on the principle of selflessness. It required men to be motivated, not by personal gain, but by love for their brothers."

Dagney heard a cold, implacable voice saying somewhere within her: Remember it – remember it well – it is not often that one can see pure evil – look at it – remember – and some day you'll find the words to name its essence . . .[1]

Ayn Rand's capitalist utopian novel, *Atlas Shrugged*, enshrines self-interest and condemns the brotherly love recommended above by Gerald Starnes, one of several hapless businessmen encountered by the novel's heroine, Dagney Taggart.

The villains of Rand's novel are unscrupulous and lazy captains of industry who inherited control over wealth from their hardworking fathers. These laggards then either squandered their fortunes in misplaced concern for the common good or preserved them by manipulating the government to squelch the competitive excellence of the true economic heroes of the day.

Written in the 1950s, Rand's fictional account endorsed libertarian capitalism at the height of the Cold War. Forty years later, the Cold War came to an abrupt end with the fall of the Soviet Union and the

[1] Ayn Rand, *Atlas Shrugged*, New American Library Edition (New York: Random House, 1957), 307.

transformation of Eastern Europe, leaving defenders of capitalism with a heady self-confidence unprecedented in the history of markets. One commentator even proclaimed, "We are all capitalist now."[2]

There was, of course, the sense that capitalism's archrival, Marxist communism, had failed and that capitalism had proved itself the superior system, judged by the standard of historical viability. However, the demise of communism alone does not explain the extent of capitalist self-esteem. That requires an understanding of the intellectual rehabilitation of capitalism that occurred during the second half of the twentieth century.

In April 1947, the economist and philosopher Friedrich Hayek brought together a small group of conservative intellectuals at the Swiss resort city of Mont Pèlerin. They gathered because the ideas of "true" nineteenth-century liberalism, what today is more frequently termed "libertarianism," were in retreat throughout the world. The claims of communism in the Soviet Union and China stood as an explicit rejection of the values of the individualism and liberty for which Hayek stood. But even more troubling was the fact that the governments of the Western world conducted their economic policy in accord with the recommendations of the economist John Maynard Keynes. Keynes's revolutionary proposal that governments should spend in deficit during economic hard times had, in the estimate of most experts, explained how the world emerged from the Great Depression. This in turn had convinced both policymakers and ordinary citizens that an activist government, both in fiscal and monetary policy, was the key to long-term prosperity. As expressed in the title of a book he had recently published, Hayek considered such policies a precursor to socialism and "the road to serfdom."[3]

It was, in fact, out of his lecture tours in the United States following the 1944 publication of *The Road to Serfdom* that Hayek decided to call that international meeting of like-minded "liberals," using that word, as he regularly did, in the nineteenth-century sense. Included in the group of thirty-six were both an older generation, among them Ludwig von Mises, Wilhelm Röpke, Karl Popper, Lionel Robbins, and Frank

[2] Michael Novak, *The Catholic Ethic and the Spirit of Capitalism* (New York: The Free Press, 1993), 101.
[3] Friedrich Hayek, *The Road to Serfdom* (Chicago: University of Chicago Press, 1944).

Knight; and a younger generation, among these Milton Friedman, Aaron Director, and George Stigler. Hayek made his purpose clear in the first sentence of his opening remarks. He reported that

If . . . a continued movement toward more government control in the greater part of the world is almost certain, this is due, more than to anything else, to the lack of a real program, or perhaps I had better say, to [a lack of] a consistent philosophy of the groups which wish to oppose it.[4]

Hayek lamented the fact that the best-known opponents of social-ism were themselves not faithful to liberal views, as they were quite willing to press for government activity in support of their own busi-ness interests. Noting the irony of his agreement with his intellectual opponent, Hayek approvingly quoted Keynes's view that

there are not many who are influenced by new theories after they are twenty-five or thirty years of age, so that the ideas which civil servants and politicians and even agitators apply are not likely to be the newest. But, soon or late, it is ideas, not vested interests, which are dangerous for good and evil.[5]

Hayek's vision was clear: "It is from this long-run point of view that we must look at our task."[6]

The Mont Pèlerin Society has grown and met some thirty times in the half-century since that original gathering, and the list of its members reads as a *Who's Who* of "free market" advocates over that time. They include government officials, Nobel laureates, newspaper columnists, university academics, and scholars at well-funded libertar-ian think tanks. There is no doubt that capitalist self-confidence at the end of the Cold War flourished at least as much because of these intellectual developments as to the downfall of communist states.

Before investigating this defense of markets, however, it is neces-sary to understand the development of what has come to be called "social ethics" in the modern world. As we shall see, much of the moral defense of markets today is based on claims that good results can arise from complex systems of human interaction even when the individuals

---

4 Friedrich Hayek, *Individualism and Economic Order* (Chicago: University of Chicago Press, 1948), 107.

5 Hayek, *Individualism*, 108, quoting John M. Keynes, *The General Theory of Employment, Interest and Money* (London: Macmillan, 1936), 383–4.

6 Hayek, *Individualism*, 108.

involved are not intending to generate those good outcomes. This sort of argument has intellectual coherence only because of a modern recognition that social ethics needs to supplement the personal ethics that moralists had earlier stressed. Following this, the chapter will outline the various moral arguments in favor of the exercise of self-interest in markets.

The Rise of Social Ethics

In the premodern world, most ethical reflection, whether religious or secular, focused on decisions made by individuals. Not only economic questions but nearly all moral issues were treated this way. Less was said about morality of social, economic, or political structures, and more attention was paid to the moral responsibility of leaders of the community, whether the monarch, local nobility, or church leaders. Nearly everyone presumed that public communal morality was (at least when things went as they should) an extension of the personal morality of the leader.

The beginning of a modern analysis of the moral logic of social structures as distinct from that of individual morality is often demarcated by the work of Thomas Hobbes (1588–1679). Hobbes proposed that the most basic legitimation for government was a reasonable decision on the part of individuals voluntarily to give their rights to the sovereign. People know that in the absence of any government, one-on-one exploitation by the physically powerful would be disastrous, worse even than a government with so extensive a power that it should be called "Leviathan."[7] Out of self-interest, Hobbes argued, individuals willingly turn over to the government their natural right to self-defense against those who would abuse them. In return, they become subjects and benefit from the government's prosecution of such abusers in its enforcement of public order. Citizens' subsequent deference to government becomes a debt, originally assumed voluntarily but now enforced by the police powers of the state. Thus, the monarch, possessing authority over their lives, rightfully operates by ethical standards different from those binding on ordinary persons. In this way Hobbes

---

[7] Thomas Hobbes, *Leviathan: or the Matter, Form, and Power of a Common-wealth Ecclesiastical and Civil* (1651) (London: Penguin Publishers, 1988).

departs from premodern notions of public morality in two ways. He argues, first, that the authority of government arises from the decision of its citizens and, second, that a different moral logic holds sway within the political realm from that which applies to individual persons.

Economically speaking, the sense of a divide between personal morality and the public good was brought to the fore in the early 1700s by Bernard Mandeville in his famous poem *Fable of the Bees*. Mandeville upset the cultured world of his day with the claim that the general prosperity of society was attributable to the selfish instincts of citizens. Individual selfishness conduced to the common good of economic prosperity. The shock was that the traditional moral condemnation of selfishness was turned on its head because of the beneficial effects of selfish action worked out through the economic system. In this way we may understand both Hobbes and Mandeville as pioneering the view that what may seem moral from the point of view of the individual person may not be moral or even beneficial when applied to the economic system.

With the twentieth-century development of sociology and anthropology, unrelated to any endorsement of capitalism, scholars came to analyze more formally the interdependence of persons and social systems. In their classic book *The Social Construction of Reality*, Peter Berger and Thomas Luckmann summarized "the sociology of knowledge" in any society. The reality of everyday life presents itself to each of us as an objective order that existed before our individual appearance on the scene and remains stubbornly resistant to our efforts to change it. Both the physical contours of the natural landscape and the social institutions within which we live confront us "as an external and coercive fact."[8] Most frequently, we don't even think of changing things because we have been socialized into the presumptions of our society that "the way we do things" is in reality "the way things need to be done." Roles and expectations created in human interaction eventually appear as only "natural."

Berger and Luckmann employ the example of two people from very different cultures who are stranded on a deserted island, each the lone survivor from a ship that sank in a fierce storm. Speaking different languages and coming from different climates, they have to

---

[8] Peter L. Berger and Thomas Luckmann, *The Social Construction of Reality: A Treatise in the Sociology of Knowledge* (New York: Anchor Books, 1966), 58.

decide everything from what qualifies as good food (they may choose the nuts familiar to one rather than the roots on which the other was raised) to how to start a fire (choosing against rubbing two sticks together in favor of striking flint). When these two people first decide to do things one way rather than another, each decision remains transparent to them and the role of humans in making that decision is clear to all. Over time with transmission from these ancestors to new generations, "the institutional world 'thickens' and 'hardens,'" becoming opaque to our gaze, cutting us off from any awareness that these patterns were and remain human creations.[9] The analysis of the "social construction of reality" provided by modern sociology makes clear that political and economic institutions – even when they seem so resistant to change – are in principle malleable. All claims by the powerful that existing institutions are in any way "natural" are undercut by anthropological studies demonstrating that, on almost every issue, it has been different – just as "naturally" – at some other time in human history or in some other place on the planet. Institutions are human creations subject to change.

From a moral point of view, an awareness of this social construction of reality generates the need for what has come to be called "social" ethics. On the one hand, if individual persons are so compellingly shaped by social meanings and structures, then even advocates of a purely personal morality will want to influence that socialization process so it will generate better rather than worse moral results. On the other hand, because social institutions lose their opacity in the penetrating light of the insight into the social construction of reality, they no longer appear to be either simply objective or immutable. Immediately, a question arises concerning the moral character of these institutions.

The Earth's gravity is not a moral issue. Why? Because there is nothing we can do about it. In the premodern world, the structures of government and the economy were similarly not moral issues for ordinary people. But as soon as people become aware of their capacity to shape them, such structures became a matter of moral deliberation. As Thomas Aquinas put it seven centuries ago, "whatever is rectifiable by reason is a matter of moral virtue."[10] Scholars debate *why* this awareness of the malleability of social institutions came to be understood

---

[9] Ibid., 59.
[10] Thomas Aquinas, *Summa Theologiae* (New York: Blackfriars, 1964), II–II, q.7, a.5.

in the West before it did in other regions of the world, but it is quite understandable that once this insight arrives, the shape of those institutions becomes a moral question, not simply a technical one.

Social ethics focuses not on the moral actions of individuals but on the form of organizations and institutions. The foundational question of social ethics isn't "How should I act?" but "How should we structure our institutions?" As individuals, we each need to act justly in economic life. But this is much more difficult if we live within unjust economic institutions. Judging the justice of institutions is a matter of social ethics. Of course, if the justice of our economic structures is to be improved, individuals and groups will need to act to make this happen. The point here, however, is that social ethics starts with questions about the character of structures.

A central insight of social ethics is that it may be morally appropriate to design social, political, or economic institutions that allow behaviors which a personal morality would not endorse or might even condemn. In this chapter, we will see how this has allowed for the moral rehabilitation of self-interest within markets. In the next chapter, we will see how critics of self-interest in markets also employ an analysis of institutions to argue a quite different case.

The Moral Arguments for Self-Interest and Markets

In analyzing Adam Smith's moral endorsement for markets, the political philosopher Joseph Cropsey observed that

> Liberal capitalism depends very much upon the dual idea of free markets and competition. It can do so only because there exists an interpretation of human nature and human life which renders competition and free markets defensible as institutions for men to live by. This is evident from the fact that in other times, and in our own time in other places, those institutions have been rejected as unfit for men to live by....[11]

Proponents of markets have indeed offered such an interpretation, and the moral arguments in favor of markets are numerous. Some are closely related to one another; some stand alone. It will be helpful to

---

[11] Joseph Cropsey, *Polity and Economy: With Further Thoughts on the Principles of Adam Smith* (South Bend, Ind.: Saint Augustine's Press, 2002), ix–x.

TABLE 3-1. *Moral Warrants for Self-Interest and Markets*

---

1. Markets encourage invention and technological change.
2. Markets create wealth for all.
3. Markets give people what they deserve.
4. Markets are just.
5. Markets reduce discrimination and bigotry.
6. Markets encourage self-interest rightly understood.
7. Markets encourage individual virtues.
8. Markets encourage political freedom and democracy.
9. Markets should not be blamed for the failures of culture.
10. An invisible hand leads self-interest to serve all.

---

review each, although any adjudication of claims here – and counter-claims in the next chapter – would extend beyond the purpose of this study.

1. Markets Encourage Invention and Technological Change

The rise of market economies over the past three centuries in the West has in large part caused the rapid development of technology. Throughout this period, because of increases of technical efficiency in production, one hour of human labor produced more wheat or chairs or machines than it did a generation earlier. Market proponents argue that although technological change is not the same as market freedom, it is exactly freedom and market-based incentives that so dramatically encourage technological change. The self-interest of those who invent new technologies is central here.

As Adam Smith noted in *The Wealth of Nations*, the key is the "division of labor" – specialization – so that a worker makes only one or two things during the work week rather than many different things. This leads the worker to develop more efficient methods of production, an investment of time and energy that would be simply inefficient if a worker were to spend only a small proportion of the total work week in each production process.

To put it more concretely, the North American subsistence farm family of the Great Plains in the mid–nineteenth century had to spend its time on many different production processes. They produced not only food of many types but also thread, cloth, clothing, soap, furniture, and so on. When specialization began to take hold, largely with the growth in the geographic size of markets caused by the arrival of the railroads, farmers focused on growing and selling food and used the proceeds to purchase the clothing, soap, and the other necessities of life they no longer had to produce themselves. Once farmers specialized in farming, there were even more agricultural inventions, driven by the creativity of individuals aiming to simplify day-long chores and adopted by the vast majority of farmers eager to purchase them.[12]

One might argue that an economy could generate technological change out of incentives other than those of economic markets. Examples here might be the scientific and technical achievements of the Mayan culture of the ninth century, the Chinese of the fifteenth century, or even the Soviet Union in the twentieth century. However, most scholars today recognize a strong correlation between market incentives and the encouragement of invention. The fact that the economies of the Maya, the Chinese, and the Soviets were left behind technologically by the far more dynamic economic systems of Western societies is often cited as evidence that economic incentives in markets drive technological change.

2. *Markets Create Wealth for All*

Perhaps the most frequent argument in favor of markets concerns their great efficiency and their ability to increase the economic well-being of broad groups of people, including the poor.[13]

As noted previously, in 1705 Bernard Mandeville shocked the staid world of moral philosophy with his *Fable of the Bees*,[14] twelve pages of doggerel verse about a prosperous colony of bees that sounded suspiciously like the England of his day. The prosperous hive has all the occupations and activities of a human society, as well as all of its vices. The key to prosperity was that "millions endeavor to supply each other's lust and vanity."[15] This prosperity is attributed to the universal

---

[12] For a review of technological change in the history of the United States, see Ross M. Robertson, *History of the American Economy*, third edition (New York: Harcourt Brace Jovanovich, 1973).

[13] For a brief yet comprehensive view over the last several centuries, see Robert E. Lucas Jr., "The Industrial Revolution: Past and Future," *The Region*, 2003 Annual Report Edition (Federal Reserve Bank of Minneapolis, May 2004), 5–20.

[14] Bernard Mandeville, *The Fable of the Bees* (Oxford: Clarendon Press, 1924).

[15] Ibid., 18.

yearning for greater riches and the attendant willingness to cut a moral corner.

> All Trades and Places knew some Cheat,
> No Calling was without Deceit.
> The Lawyers, of whose Art the Basis
> Was raising Feuds and splitting Cases,. . . .
> Physicians valu'd Fame and Wealth
> Above the drooping Patient's Health.[16]

Mandeville's claim was that it was private vice that generated public well-being.

> Thus Vice nurs'd Ingenuity,
> Which join'd with Time and Industry,
> Had carry'd Life's Conveniences,
> Its real Pleasures, Comforts, Ease,
> To such a Height, the very Poor
> Liv'd better than the Rich before.[17]

To make his point more vividly, Mandeville arranges for Jove in heaven to magically rid the prosperous hive of all the vices against which its spiritual leaders and ordinary citizens had so long railed. Everyone turns honest, causing the list of the unemployed to grow dramatically, including lawyers, jailers, locksmiths, clergymen, and that vast array of ordinary workers who produce things that the bees in their erstwhile vanity used to crave. The hive loses its economic prosperity and a good portion of its population, rending it unable even to defend itself against its enemies. The *Fable*'s moral is added in a poetic summary at the end:

> Fools only strive
> To make a Great an Honest Hive.
> T' enjoy the World's Conveniences
> Be fam'd in War, yet live in Ease,
> Without great Vices, is a vain
> Eutopia seated in the Brain.
> Fraud, Luxury and Pride must live
> While we the Benefits receive.[18]

[16] Ibid., 20.
[17] Ibid., 26.
[18] Ibid., 36.

Mandeville's conclusion was that private vices bring public benefit, a claim that elicited a lively condemnation of his work. Adam Smith attacked Mandeville's argument as "licentious" and "wholly pernicious," and similar reactions arose from other lights of British society, including Bishop Berkeley, Francis Hutcheson, and Edward Gibbon. A grand jury in Middlesex condemned the work as a public nuisance.[19]

It must be admitted that Mandeville's claim that the poor lived better than the rich did previously refers to their material conditions and not to other elements of overall well-being, such as social status and self-respect, which do not always correlate with monetary income. Nonetheless, economic well-being is morally important, and even several Christian theologians have recently argued for the moral attractiveness of the "culture of affluence" in capitalism.[20] But even those who would provide a less-ringing endorsement of affluence should recognize that the economic history of the past 300 years has definitely ended the traditional premodern expectation that the people of one century would be about as well off economically as their descendants in the next. Rising economic productivity generates rising economic well-being over time even for average citizens.

Perhaps the best way to recognize this is to consider what has happened to the average wage of ordinary workers (technically termed "unskilled labor") in the United States since the founding of the nation. (Examining this average wage is more telling than focusing on a more general statistic such as total income per capita, because the latter averages in the well-being of wealthy property owners with that of ordinary workers.) Adjusting for inflation, the average wage of an ordinary worker in 1776 doubled by 1810, doubled again by 1888, and doubled again in 1934 and 1955.[21]

In addition, market proponents argue that when government *does* need to step into the economy – for example, to correct the market failure represented by air pollution from industrial smokestacks – it

[19] Gertrude Himmelfarb, "The Idea of Compassion: The British vs. the French Enlightenment," *The Public Interest* 145 (Fall 2001), 3–25.

[20] See, for example, John R. Schneider, *The Good of Affluence: Seeking God in a Culture of Wealth* (Grand Rapids, Mich.: William B. Eerdmans, 2002).

[21] Samuel H. Williamson, "An Index of the Wage of Unskilled Labor from 1774 to the Present," Economic History Services (March 17, 2003), URL: http://www.eh.net/hmit/databases/unskilledwage/

should employ "market-based" methods, such as tradeable pollution permits. The use of such methods is more efficient and eventuates in greater overall wealth because, at whatever level of expenditure society chooses, it will reduce pollution more than any other approach. Moreover, market incentives show greater respect for the freedom of individuals than do government-enforced mandates to address the problem by one and only one method.

Another reason for allowing individuals to seek their own interests in the market is articulated in Frederick Hayek's insight into the limitations of knowledge. Every situation facing each person is unique, and no government can possibly know the details of each of them better than the particular persons involved. One of the beauties of the exercise of self-interest in markets is that every individual is allowed, even encouraged, "to take advantage of those peculiar opportunities which chance has thrown in his way but not in that of others."[22]

For Hayek, the market is a sort of "discovery procedure"[23] whose efficiency governments cannot rival. Because individuals know the local situation and can best decide when to initiate or, more important, abandon economic initiatives, the role of government is to facilitate this sort of free interaction. In Hayek's words, "in a free society the general good consists principally in the facilitating of the pursuit of unknown individual purposes."[24]

The vitality and prosperity of market societies depend on this attractive and productive possibility facing every individual. Markets receive a moral endorsement because of the increase in economic well-being they generate not only for the wealthy but for ordinary people as well.

3. Markets Give People What They Deserve

Advocates of markets often claim that the exercise of self-interest in markets is morally justifiable because markets give people what they deserve. Economists as social scientists have typically avoided moral claims, but in a famous episode at the end of the nineteenth century, the U.S. economist John Bates Clark asserted that the various

---

[22] Hayek, *Law, Legislation and Liberty*, Vol. 2, *The Mirage of Social Justice* (Chicago: University of Chicago Press, 1973), 10.

[23] Ibid.

[24] Ibid., 1.

participants to economic production – workers, managers, owners of capital – are each paid their "marginal product" and this is indeed a morally just compensation because it is based on their actual economic contributions. Economists were quick to criticize this insertion of moral analysis into economic science itself, but the view of the justice of compensation in accord with marginal contribution is widely held today by many who have studied economics and by many economists in their role as citizens.[25]

Related to this claim, others have argued that markets give to economic actors the economic return they deserve and that markets are morally more appropriate distributors of the output of goods and services in an economy than any conceivable human decision-making process embodied in government could ever be. Here there is a general sense that hard work, initiative, education, and other forms of forgoing current pleasure in order to increase future income are all moral justifications for market outcomes. This, of course, resonates well with the kind of advice most parents give to their children: Work hard and plan ahead, and you'll be better off. And this, many advocates of markets argue, is exactly the kind of behavior that markets encourage.

4. Markets Are Just

One of the central moral claims in favor of markets is that they provide the only appropriate system for a just economic interaction among individuals. Here markets are contrasted with economic decisions made by governments, usually national governments.

This is the major claim of libertarians in contemporary debates about markets and morality: Only a "minimal" state will respect individuals' rights to control the things they have justly produced or acquired in the market. Robert Nozick,[26] in *Anarchy, State and Utopia*, probably the best-known libertarian treatise of the twentieth century, argues that three simple principles cover the issue of justice in what persons own.

---

[25] See John Bates Clark, *The Philosophy of Wealth: Economic Principles Newly Formulated* (1886), (New York: A. M. Kelley, 1967). For a standard economic critique of Clark on this issue, see Joseph A. Schumpeter, *History of Economic Analysis* (New York: Oxford University Press, 1954), 870.

[26] Nozick, *Anarchy, State and Utopia* (Oxford: Blackwell, 1974), 151.

The first is that any acquisition of something from nature, where it has been owned by no one, needs to be done justly. Here Nozick defers to John Locke's view, arguing that the appropriation from nature by individual owners has been just because the system of private ownership has improved the lot of even those who did not themselves make an appropriation.[27] In the modern world, the vast majority of things people want are already owned by somebody else, and thus this principle of original acquisition from nature does not often come into play in daily life. The second is the principle of just transfer, which states that an individual justly receives and possesses anything that another has voluntarily transferred, as long as the other possessed that thing justly before the transfer. This is the justice of the typical market transaction, where you own something and voluntarily decide to transfer its ownership to another, usually because of an offer to transfer something else to you in return. The third is the principle of rectification of injustice: If anyone violates either of the first two principles, some sort of rectification must be made to those harmed by the violation.

Because all of the things anyone might own are covered by these three principles, according to Nozick "they raise the question of what, if anything, the state and its officials may do."[28] Because citizens have the right to keep the things they have justly acquired, governments do not have a right to take away any part of these holdings.

Thus, for libertarians, market transactions are the model for just interactions of persons in all areas of life, and governments typically violate justice when they alter the outcomes of market interactions. The market, where individuals must persuade the other to engage in an exchange with them, remains the most just of human institutions. Antedating Nozick, Friedrich Hayek argued, as we have seen, that no

[27] John Locke himself relaxed his original limitation on how much can be justly appropriated – that there must remain in the commons "enough and as good." John Locke, *Two Treatises of Government*, Chapter 5 (New York: Cambridge University Press, 1960), 33. Locke argued that of all the wealth of his day, less than 1% was attributable to nature and the rest to human labor. Nozick broadens the argument to claim that this "Lockean proviso" of enough and as good left in the commons is equivalent to a requirement that those who cannot appropriate (because the appropriators do so first) are not harmed, compared with their baseline position prior to any appropriation. Nozick argues that the private-property system is so productive that even the non–propertied class was benefited by the process. Nozick, *Anarchy*, 178.
[28] Nozick, *Anarchy*, ix.

government can know what is good for an individual better than the individual can. Thus both from the perspective of the right to act and the competence to do so, it is the individual who should decide. The government should limit itself to making and enforcing only general rules.

Man has developed rules of conduct not because he knows but because he does not know what all the consequences of a particular action will be and the most characteristic feature of morals and law as we know them is therefore that they consist of rules to obey irrespective of the known effects of the particular action.[29]

5. Markets Reduce Discrimination and Bigotry

Proponents of markets praise the slow but steady historical move away from tribal morality toward the abstract and general rules of conduct that regulate interactions in modern life. Hayek reminds his readers that they should not lament the loss of fellow feeling in that transition but rather appreciate the overthrow of those "special rules which allow the individual to harm the stranger if it serves the interest of his group."[30] Markets are the best representation of this sort of respectful but largely impersonal relation among people, and they are attractive for the way they encourage a nondiscriminatory treatment of others.

As argued by Milton Friedman discussing discrimination based on race, religion, or other characteristics, "the man who exercises discrimination pays a price for doing so."[31] The market militates against such biases because it "separates economic efficiency from irrelevant characteristics."[32] Any person or business that through bigotry will avoid hiring some group of potential employees or selling to some group of potential customers will be disadvantaged economically and eventually will be replaced by those more economically efficient firms that do not hold and exercise such prejudices.

Discrimination and bigotry are economically inefficient, and markets discourage such beliefs and practices.

[29] Hayek, *Law*, 2:20–1.
[30] Hayek, *Law*, 2:148.
[31] Milton Friedman, *Capitalism and Freedom* (Chicago: University of Chicago Press, 1962), 110.
[32] Ibid., 109.

6. Markets Encourage Self-Interest Rightly Understood

Many proponents admit that markets allow the sway of self-interest but argue that this is not a "dog-eat-dog" form of self-interest. Rather, markets encourage a "rightly understood" self-interest, something morally far more attractive. As one argument has put it, "the system works best by incentives, by the flowering of natural virtues, by candor and open communication, by a sense of dignity and belonging."[33] The business system itself depends on a spirit of cooperation and a mutual respect between producers and customers, employers and employees.

This notion of self-interest "rightly understood" is borrowed from Alexis de Tocqueville, the nineteenth-century French observer of American culture, who noted that "the inhabitants of the United States almost always manage to combine their advantage with that of their fellow citizens."[34] Some have called this "an egalitarian conception of virtue," in the sense that it does not call for the highest levels of self-sacrifice but nonetheless "directs the passions toward the virtues crucial to human good."[35]

7. Markets Encourage Individual Virtues

Some proponents of markets go beyond the claim that markets depend on the virtues of individual economic actors to argue that markets actively encourage many particular virtues. Firms will be more profitable if they treat their customers with integrity and an attitude of service. Markets reward ingenuity, hard work, and vision. As one recent study has put it,

Free markets, in principle, foster many values and practices that lend themselves to just social structures by respecting human nature. . . . Market activity can foster specific virtues. Trust, courage, thrift, industriousness, and creativity are all encouraged in a free-market system.[36]

---

[33] Lay Commission on Catholic Society Teaching under the U.S. Economy, *Toward the Future: Catholic Social Thought and the U.S. Economy: A Lay Letter*, New York: American Catholic Committee (1984), 20.

[34] Ibid., 21.

[35] Ibid., 22.

[36] Anthony J. Santelli Jr., Jeffrey Sikkenga, Robert A. Sirico, Steven Yates, and Gloria Zúñiga, *The Free Person and the Free Economy* (Lanham, Md.: Lexington Books, 2002), 124.

This argument is a modern version of an older assertion known as the "*doux commerce* thesis." This notion, which dates to Montesquieu, Hume, Condorcet, and others, asserts that economic relationships within a market tend to offset historic hostilities with gentler manners and cordiality, even if only out of the self-interest of the participants.[37] One need only look to the level of economically driven cooperation today between the historic enemies France and Germany to understand the civilizing power of self-interest in markets.

8. Markets Encourage Political Freedom and Democracy

Market proponents argue that economic freedom is an essential part of the broader human freedom necessary for human happiness. Here Milton Friedman is among the most articulate in defending the economic freedom to pursue one's interest.

> On the one hand, freedom in economic arrangements is itself a component of freedom broadly understood, so economic freedom is an end in itself. In the second place, economic freedom is also an indispensable means toward the achievement of political freedom.[38]

From this perspective, then, markets should remain as "free" as possible not only out of a concern for efficiency and productivity but also because allowing this freedom serves a broader moral need for freedom in human life. Economic freedom is itself a moral good.

A further argument in favor of allowing individuals to exercise their self-interests in markets is one more associated with political theory than with economic. Charles Murray has argued that since the earliest days of Greek and Roman democracy, "republics collapse when a faction is able to use the state to impose its vision of the good on the rest of society."[39] Murray's argument here is related to that provided by both

---

[37] As Albert Hirschman has found in the work of Samuel Ricard in 1704, "through commerce, man learns to deliberate, to be honest, to acquire manners, to be prudent and reserved in both talk and action. Sensing the necessity to be wise and honest in order to succeed, he flees vice, or at least his demeanor exhibits decency and seriousness so as not to arouse any adverse judgment on the part of present and future acquaintances." Albert O. Hirschman, *Rival Views of Market Society and Other Recent Essays* (Cambridge, Mass.: Harvard University Press, 1992), 108.

[38] Milton Friedman, *Capitalism*, 8.

[39] Charles Murray, *In Pursuit of Happiness and Good Government* (San Francisco: Institute for Contemporary Studies, 1994), 140.

Buchanan and Hayek in Chapter 2. If one gives the government the power to interfere with the exercise of individuals' self-interest, the natural tendency in democracy is for abuse to follow. "As time goes on, and as the limits on what is permissible for government to do are loosened, there will be no defense against any number of bad things being done in the name of good."[40]

In their annual report *Economic Freedom of the World*, James Gwartney and Robert Lawson calculate changes in the level of economic freedom in each of the nations of the world. Not only do the data show that greater economic freedom leads to higher incomes, for both the rich and poor, but, they argue "political rights (e.g., free and fair elections) and civil liberties (e.g., freedom of speech) go hand in hand with economic freedom."[41] Markets encourage political freedom and democracy.

9. Markets Should Not Be Blamed for the Failures of Culture

A frequent argument in favor of markets is that critics mistakenly blame markets for problems that are actually caused by the broader culture. To take but one example, many Christian proponents of markets are critical of rampant "consumerism" – defined as "a culture's obsession with shopping and buying."[42] Some thoughtful commentators lament this distortion of basic human values but go on to observe that "usually, such a situation is blamed on the market economy. Yet if examined carefully consumerism is really a malfunction of the human heart. It is the idolatry of wealth."[43]

Production and distribution in market society do "little if anything" to foster consumerism. "To argue that it does is similar to arguing that we should blame the alcohol and not the alcoholic."[44] Others have even argued that the problem of corruption in Enron, Tyco, and

---

[40] Ibid., 141.

[41] James Gwartney and Robert Lawson, *Economic Freedom of the World* (Vancouver: Frasier, 2004), 22.

[42] Patricia Donahue-White, Stephen J. Grabill, Christopher Westley, and Gloria Zúñiga, *Human Nature and the Discipline of Economics* (Lanham, Md.: Lexington Books, 2002), 98.

[43] Ibid.

[44] Gregory M.A. Gronbacher, "The Human Economy: Neither Right nor Left; A Response to Daniel Rush Finn" in *Journal of Markets and Morality* 2 (Fall 1999), 268.

other corporations was not the lack of legal safeguards but the "ethos" of corruption, a thoroughly cultural problem.[45]

From this perspective, a life in business has a moral dignity to it, contrary to traditional criticism of business and commerce. The key to sustaining and deepening that moral dimension in the economy is not the implementation of more legislative norms but rather the strengthening of cultural influences: religious, educational, civic, and otherwise. As William McGurn has put it reflecting on freedom, "if the culture does not cultivate a proper view of that freedom – in sharp contrast to the radical autonomy that leads only to self-gratification – we shall end up destroying the virtues upon which our markets and the affluence they create rest."[46]

10. An Invisible Hand Leads Self-Interest to Serve All

A final argument endorsing the self-interest of markets is related to Adam Smith's notion of the "invisible hand." This idea has had a life far beyond any that Smith himself could have dreamed. The phrase appears only once in his *Wealth of Nations*, a volume of nearly a thousand pages, and Smith applies it only to the beneficial effects of investment when done in one's home country rather than abroad. But the notion correlates with the broader claim within Smith's work that self-interest plays a positive role within the economy. In his classic phrase,

it is not from the benevolence of the butcher, the brewer or the baker, that we expect our dinner, but from their regard to their own interest. We address ourselves not to their humanity but to their self love, and never talk to them of our own necessities but of their advantages.[47]

Smith's point here, of course, is that when we walk into the bakery we offer money in exchange for the bread we want to bring home, making an offer the baker will want to accept, with both of us acting out of self-interest. Although Smith does not make the point explicitly, the implicit intention is clear and has been repeated by proponents of markets ever since. Self-interest has a moral attractiveness when it is a

45 William McGurn, in Rebecca M. Blank and William McGurn, *Is the Market Moral? A Dialogue on Religion, Economics and Justice* (Washington, D.C.: Brookings Institution Press, 2004), 140.

46 Ibid., 87.

47 Adam Smith, *The Wealth of Nations* (New York: Modern Library, 1937), 14.

servant of a process that both gives productive employment to those at the bakery and provides nourishment for consumers at home. The notion of the "invisible hand," as extended by proponents after Smith's day, broadens this insight. It argues that the general (some even say universal) result of the exercise of self-interest in markets is that the good of all will be ultimately served. This indeed is a morally attractive view of self-interest, as it encompasses nearly all the more particular arguments in favor of self-interest in markets identified previously.

Conclusion

Debates over the morality of economic exchange are ancient. Most proponents of markets, and of self-interested activity within them, are well aware of the conflict with traditional moral advice against egoism and greed, but they argue that because of the institutionally mediated effects of self-interest in markets, self-interested action deserves our moral endorsement. This is indeed an argument in social ethics, an argument about the character of our institutions that does not simply apply norms for personal morality to social structures. It is different (at least for most market proponents) from the kind of advice they might give to their children about how to treat siblings or classmates.

Although the moral logic of this difference is usually left unstated, it represents a critical shift in moral analysis in the modern world. From the perspective of market advocates, "purity" of intentions – whether one is a follower of Jesus, Socrates, or the Buddha – may work well in private morality but can cause confusion and poverty when applied to our major economic and political institutions. A growing awareness of this difference between individual and institutional morality undergirds the moral endorsement of markets in the past three centuries.

Of course, critics of this growing moral endorsement of self-interest in markets disagree, and to those disagreements we now turn.

4

The Moral Critique of Self-Interest and Markets

> The gentlest creatures are fierce when they have young to provide for, and in that wolfish society the struggle for bread borrowed a peculiar desperation from the tenderest sentiments.

> For the sake of those dependent on him, a man might not want to but *must* plunge into the foul fight – cheat, overreach, supplant, defraud, buy below worth and sell above, break down the business by which his neighbor fed his young ones, tempt men to buy what they ought not and to sell what they should not, grind his laborers, sweat his debtors, cozen his creditors.[1]

Edward Bellamy's 1888 socialist utopian novel, *Looking Backward*, condemns the structures of capitalism. As the clergyman, Mr. Barton, argues above in the fictional year 2000, the citizens of the capitalist nineteenth century were not by nature more evil than their socialist descendants 112 years later. Rather it was the insecurity of the market economy, continually threatening financial ruin, that produced the selfish, anti-social behaviors that proponents of capitalism mistakenly believe are inevitable outcomes of human nature. Unlike Ayn Rand's novels, Bellamy's work has no great heroes, only reasonable people who argue that it is not human nature that makes capitalism so harsh but capitalism that presses men and women to be so harsh with each other.

---

[1] Edward Bellamy, *Looking Backward* [1888], (New York: New American Library, 1960), 185.

Bellamy's novel describes a postcapitalist world that is not only egalitarian but also wealthier than the capitalism it supplanted. Economic well-being in any society depends on the production of goods and services that are ultimately useful to people. In Bellamy's socialist world, everyone received a handsome annual allotment of funds to live on. This increase in national prosperity was paid for by the now-productive work of people who in the earlier capitalist world had been engaged in unproductive but "necessary" occupations. In Bellamy's twenty-first century Boston there was no need for accountants or financial advisors to plan for retirement, attorneys or judges to litigate disputes among capitalist firms, police or prison guards to apprehend and punish criminals driven by poverty, unemployed laborers unable to find jobs, retail clerks competing among themselves to persuade consumers to buy goods they really don't need, and a myriad of other workers in a capitalist system who do not produce the goods or services people want. In this, Bellamy combines two great traditions of critique against self-interest and capitalist markets. He argues not only that economic selfishness is morally repugnant but also that it is economically profligate, inefficiently wasting both material resources and human energy in the dog-eat-dog competition of capitalism.

To investigate this moral critique of self-interest in markets, this chapter first addresses the notion of self-interest and then turns to the various arguments employed in that critique.

What Is Self-Interest?

As we saw in Chapter 3, the economic view of self-interest today arises out of the nineteenth-century utilitarian origins of the economist's view of human decision making. Mainstream economics today presumes that every action taken by the individual is self-interested, in the sense that it pursues some interest of the self. Thus, both Mother Teresa and the thief in Calcutta are described as pursuing their self-interest, even though she lives in extreme poverty to serve the poor while he preys upon them. This definition is logically consistent and arises out of the mainstream economist's interest in avoiding moral judgments about human action within the science, but it has severe shortcomings that are often overlooked.

The dominant economic view of human choice is a version of "psychological egoism," the doctrine that all human action is inevitably egoistic, oriented toward the benefit of the actor. As William Frankena explains, psychological egoism claims that "each of us is always seeking his own greatest good, whether this is conceived of as pleasure, happiness, knowledge, power, self-realization. . . ."[2] The claim of psychological egoism is an empirical one – that people do act this way – with the explicit intention to avoid any judgment as to whether this fact of life is good or bad from a moral point of view. Thus, the psychological egoist is ready to find some self-interest to explain all decisions, even apparently altruistic ones. Even the soldier who jumps on the live grenade to save the lives of his nearby buddies is interpreted as doing so in order that he might be well thought of by them and by everyone else who hears the story.

In contrast to psychological egoism, ethical egoism is the moral argument that "an individual's one and only basic obligation is to promote for himself the greatest possible balance of good over evil."[3] Ethical egoism says nothing empirically about how many people in the world act this way but rather proposes that all should do so. In reality, very few people endorse ethical egoism. At the same time, however, it is clear that those who endorse psychological egoism will be less skeptical of ethical egoism than others. If every human action inevitably furthers the interest of the actor, there is no great moral shame in arguing that every action *ought* to do so. Thus, economists who really believe the psychological egoism of their model of human decision making may thereby be more disposed to also choose ethical egoism as a moral approach to economic life.

Critics often find explanations proposed by psychological egoism to be both unpersuasive and harmful, for three reasons.[4]

The first problem is that psychological egoism is fundamentally a tautology. It is not an empirical statement about the world, but rather

---

[2] William K. Frankena, *Ethics*, second edition (Englewood Cliffs, N.J.: Prentice-Hall, 1973), 21.

[3] Ibid., 18.

[4] A fourth, not to be investigated here, is the conviction that economics as a profession either attracts people who are more selfish than the average or actually leads people to become more selfish. See Robert Rowthorn, "Ethics and Economics: An Economist's View, in *Economics and Ethics?*, Peter Groenewegen, ed. (London and New York: Routledge, 1996), 19.

it simply *defines* all human decision making as egoistic. It fails the test of "falsifiability" proposed by the philosopher Karl Popper to separate scientifically meaningful hypotheses (statements about the world) from mere definitions.[5] According to Popper, if there is no conceivable event that, should it occur, would disprove an hypothesis, then in actuality the hypothesis says nothing about the real world and is scientifically vacuous. If every conceivable human action can be explained by self-interest, then self-interest explains nothing. As Amartya Sen has put it, this view of self-interest creates an "enchanted world of definitions."[6]

The second problem with psychological egoism is that, for most people, making a distinction between Mother Teresa and the thief – between vice and virtue – is critically important in understanding the world empirically. Any description of the world that cannot distinguish saint from sinner, martyr from murderer, altruism from selfishness is like a summer landscape painted with only half the colors of the palette. There is some correspondence to reality, and for some purposes – Are the flowers to the right or left of the trees? – the depiction is sufficiently accurate. The problem comes when one employs that depiction in situations where its shortcomings render it a distortion. Leading a moral life is difficult and at various times requires the subordination of one's interests to those of others. As a result, the economist's assertion that all action is self-interested is a fundamentally distorted description of human life.

Thus, the second of these two objections points out that the claims of psychological egoism are false, while the first asserts that, being based on pure definition, the claims are vacuous. As Jane Mansbridge has put it, "some rational choice theorists equivocate on this point, most of the time making the false claim, and backing off to a vacuous claim under critical fire."[7]

---

5 Karl Popper, *Conjectures and Refutations: The Growth of Scientific Knowledge* (London: Routledge, 1963).

6 Amartya K. Sen, "Rational Fools: A Critique of the Behavioral Foundations of Economic Theory," first published in H. Harris, ed., *Scientific Models and Men* (London: Oxford University Press, 1978), 317–44; reprinted in Jane J. Mansbridge, ed., *Beyond Self-Interest* (Chicago: University of Chicago Press, 1990), 29.

7 Jane J. Mansbridge, "The Rise and Fall of Self-Interest and the Explanation of Political Life," in *Beyond Self-Interest*, Jane J. Mansbridge, ed. (Chicago: University of Chicago Press, 1990), 21.

A third problem in psychological egoism is pointed out by James White in his complaint that the ordinary meaning of self-interest as "selfishness" will in the end be too strong; people won't keep in mind that the technical economic notion of self-interest can include concern for others. As he puts it, "one cannot habitually think of human actions in such terms ... without in fact universalizing the ordinary rather than the technical meaning. The result is to validate both selfishness and the desire to acquire and consume."[8]

Acknowledging these difficulties, this book employs the terms "self-interest" and "self-interested" in the generic manner that economic science does. That is, self-interest is here understood as the interest of the self, which could include either narrowly selfish or broadly altruistic goals held by the actor. The phrase "narrow self-interest" refers to actions in which the self (perhaps including a few loved ones near the self) is the intended beneficiary of action. Thus, when actions are taken in the interest of others but the *intention* is to serve the well-being of the actor, that action is described as narrowly self-interested, even if it also redounds to the benefit of others.

Some have tried to employ other terms such as "enlightened self-interest," or what Alexis de Toqueville more than a century ago called self-interest "rightly understood," in order to bridge the moral gap that narrow self-interest within markets typically creates. The sentiment behind both of these phrases is that we can best serve our own narrow self-interest in the market by satisfying the interests of other market actors with whom we deal. The classic formulation here is provided in Adam Smith's notion that we enter the bakery and appeal to the baker's self-interest. In practical terms, we offer money to obtain goods we seek and do not appeal to the merchant's concern for our needs.

For Smith, this commercial interaction that generates dinner is understood on both sides as furthering each person's narrow self-interest. However, the defense of capitalism, especially in the United States, adds a twist to this notion as de Toqueville described in his famous *Democracy in America*:

The American moralists do not profess that men ought to sacrifice themselves for their fellow creatures because it is noble to make such sacrifices. ... They

[8] James Boyd White, "Economics and Law: Two Cultures in Tension," in *Tennessee Law Review* 54 (1987): 171.

therefore do not deny that every man may follow his own interests, but they endeavor to prove that it is in the interest of every man to be virtuous.[9]

Twentieth-century defenders of capitalism, even some working from a religious perspective, argued that de Tocqueville's "egalitarian conception of virtue" eventuates in a moral warrant for capitalism.[10]

The central problem with the notions of "enlightened" self-interest and self-interest "rightly understood" is that the relation between the interest of others and the interest of the self is left confused, or perhaps intentionally ambivalent.

On the one hand, these two phrases could refer simply to a long-term calculation of narrow self-interest. I hold your interests as important to me, but only to the extent that my own long-run narrow self-interest will be better served by doing so. At the point where it will not be, I no longer care about your interests. In this form, "enlightened" or "properly understood" self-interest is simply a shrewder and longer-term calculation of narrow self-interest than a naïve egoist might undertake. Most persons of moral conviction would be quite reluctant to buy into a defense of markets if doing so were acknowledged as being only a form of egoism.

On the other hand, these phrases could mean that one's own narrow interests happen to be well served as a by-product of an authentic, independent interest in the other, whose well-being is valuable to me independent of its impact on my own. If the empirical situation is such that markets do indeed reward this kind of "self-interest," market proponents will have a strong moral case. The efforts expended by many successful capitalist firms to serve their customers well are often cited as evidence of self-interest rightly understood.

However, to question the accuracy of this bold assumption, one need only think of the difference between the status of customers and that of employees in a typical modern corporation. Because of competition with other firms and because few firms have more customers than they want, the corporation works hard to treat the customer well in order to create more business for itself. At the same time, because of

---

[9] Alexis de Tocqueville, *Democracy in America* (1835), vol. 2 (New York: Penguin, 2001), Chapter 7.

[10] Lay Commission on Catholic Society Teaching and the U.S. Economy, *Toward the Future: Catholic Social Thought and the U.S. Economy: A Lay Letter* (New York: American Catholic Committee, 1984), 22.

competition among workers and because firms can in most situations
hire more or different workers at about the same wage, firms often
enter into hard-nosed labor negotiations in determining wages and
working conditions in which the conflicts between the interests of the
firm and those of the employees are clear. It is important to note that
this conflict exists even though there is a general long-term identity of
interests between firms and employees that is often hidden amid the
short-term strife.

Those proponents of capitalism who advocate the view that valuing the interest of the other also happens to serve one's own interests rarely discuss the relation between employers and employees.
The critical question is this: What will the firm do if its narrow long-
term interests do *not* coincide with those of employees or those of any
other group with whom it deals, for example suppliers or customers?
Although defenders of markets and capitalism argue that dog-eat-dog
self-interest is not required, they never suggest that the firm should sacrifice its narrow long-term self-interest. When such an ultimate question is asked it is hard to distinguish "enlightened" self-interest or
self-interest "rightly understood" from a careful long-term calculation
of narrow self-interest.

This incoherence in the notion of self-interest rightly understood
was seen by de Tocqueville himself as a kind of morally inspired self-
deception prevalent in America, even though this side of de Tocqueville's thought is rarely noted by those market proponents who
employ his views. He observed that

in the United States as well as elsewhere people are sometimes seen to give
way to those disinterested and spontaneous impulses that are natural to man:
but the Americans seldom admit that they yield to emotions of this kind.[11]

His point is that Americans are both more and less virtuous than they
might otherwise be because they join in a broadly shared and carefully
cultivated double delusion. One delusion asserts that serving first the
interest of others does in fact serve one's own interests. Although this
is frequently true as producers strive to offer what consumers desire,
it is also frequently false as, for example, each year Madison Avenue
advertising dollars strive cleverly to induce consumers to purchase

[11] Tocqueville, *Democracy*, Chapter 7.

things they otherwise would be less inclined to buy. The other delusion asserts that it is morally praiseworthy to serve the interest of others even if your only intention is to further your own interests. Although few ethical positions object if service to others happens to redound to one's own benefit, only the rarely endorsed "ethical egoism"[12] would defend the moral principle that the right thing to do is to seek one's own interest.

Defenders of this approach, however, value the first delusion because it turns down the volume on the prideful inclination to put self before others. They also appreciate that the second turns down the volume on the moral exhortation to reach for a higher level of virtue, because this so often leads to a call for inefficient government regulation of moral excess in the market. Illusory or not, the more people who believe in "self-interest rightly understood," they hold, the more humane will be the economic system.

The moral endorsement of enlightened or rightly understood self-interest, then, plays an important but ambiguous role in the debate over the morality of capitalism. On the one hand it asserts that self-interest is a morally positive force, leaving critics of capitalism to complain about the incoherence and dishonesty of the claim. On the other hand, it advises the economically powerful to engage in virtuous behavior, but defined in a way that few moral traditions – religious or secular – would recognize. "Be willing to set aside your own interests in the short run, but be assured this will actually further your interests in the long run." In commenting on Benjamin Franklin's endorsement of a similar view, Max Weber called this a "utilitarian" conception of virtue.[13] Perhaps de Tocqueville's own summary is still the best:

If the principle of interest as rightly understood were to sway the whole world, extraordinary virtues would doubtless be more rare: but I think that gross depravity would also then be less common. The principle of interest rightly understood perhaps prevents men from rising far above the level of mankind,

---

[12] Frankena, *Ethics*, 18.

[13] Max Weber, *The Protestant Ethic and The Sprit of Capitalism* (Chicago: Fitzroy Dearborn Publishers, 2001). Utilitarians themselves would object that in true utilitarianism the self counts no more than any other person, and thus self-interest cannot suffice for the moral life.

TABLE 4-1. *Moral Criticisms of Self-Interest and Markets*

11. Markets generate an unjust distribution of income and well-being.
12. Markets threaten the environment.
13. Markets need enforcement of basic justice.
14. Market outcomes are not deserved.
15. Markets should not be exonerated by blaming culture.
16. Markets encourage greed.
17. Markets undermine culture and their own moral foundations.
18. Conservatives exaggerate the problems created by government.

but a great number of other men, who were falling far below it, are caught and restrained by it.[14]

Proponents of capitalism argue that within a well-functioning culture, more capitalists would heed their advice and be "caught and restrained."[15] Critics point to those many economically powerful persons who pay only lip service to the advice but benefit from the moral endorsement it provides to a capitalist system that so often handsomely rewards narrow self-interest.

The Moral Critique of Self-Interest and Markets

The accusations against the exercise of self-interest in markets are diverse, so it will be helpful to move through them one at a time.

1. Markets Generate an Unjust Distribution of Income and Well-Being

Critics argue that proponents of markets significantly exaggerate their capacity to increase economic well-being, especially that of the poor.

A first line of criticism questions the very measuring stick employed by proponents of markets when they claim that economic well-being is increasing. Fundamental economic measures, such the "gross domestic product" (GDP), aim to measure the sum total of economic activity

---

[14] Tocqueville, *Democracy*, Chapter 7.

[15] Here the proponents of "self-interest rightly understood" aim to align the impact of culture with the *"doux commerce"* effects of modern capitalism itself, that creates "a set of compatible psychological attitudes and moral dispositions, that are both desirable in themselves and conducive to the further expansion of the system." Albert O. Hirschman, *The Rhetoric of Reaction: Perversity, Futility, Jeopardy* (Cambridge, Mass.: Harvard University Press, 1991), 109.

in a nation. Per capita GDP (total GDP divided by the number of persons in the nation) has been rising regularly for more than two centuries in the United States and Europe. Critics argue, however, that many of the expenditures measured in GDP are actually unfortunate necessities and do not represent any increase in well-being. When you choose to install an additional lock on your front door, this expenditure is measured as an increase in GDP, but, in fact, your doing so is usually only an attempt to regain a sense of security you once had. Similarly, extra expenditure on gasoline burned in traffic jams, air purifiers to counteract the effects of smog, and a host of other goods and services are "defensive" and do not represent real increases in economic well-being. Thus, GDP and GDP per capita are faulty measures of well-being. A number of efforts have been made to correct this problem, with more moderate assessments finding that per capita economic well-being has risen, but much more slowly than per capita GDP would indicate.[16] One thorough revision of the measuring stick has found that economic well-being per capita in the United States has actually been falling for the past few decades.[17]

A second line of critique argues that even if one accepts the usual economic measures of well-being, there is a growing inequality between the poor and the rich, both within individual nations and internationally. In the United States, income equality has been rising since 1968.[18]

A very concrete way of understanding the extent of the inequality of wealth in the United States is to map the existing distribution of wealth of the nation onto the board of "Monopoly," that ubiquitous childhood board game. If the properties on the Monopoly board were owned in proportion to the distribution of wealth in the United States, the wealthiest one-half of 1 percent of U.S. citizens would own Boardwalk

[16] See, for example, William Nordhaus and James Tobin, "Is Growth Obsolete?" in *Economic Growth,* National Bureau of Economic Research, General Series 96E (New York: Columbia University Press, 1972).

[17] Early work on the "Index of Sustainable Economic Welfare" appears as the appendix in Herman E. Daly and John B. Cobb Jr., *For the Common Good: Redirecting the Economy Toward Community, the Environment, and a Sustainable Future* (Boston: Beacon Press, 1989). A current version, now called the "genuine progress indicator" (GPI) is available at redefiningprogress.org.

[18] U.S. Bureau of the Census, *Current Population Reports* (Washington, D.C.: U.S. Bureau of the Census, 1996).

and Park Place as well as the next two most expensive properties on the board. The next wealthiest 4.5 percent of the population would own Pacific Avenue, all three yellow properties, all three red properties, and New York Avenue, the most expensive orange property on the board. The next wealthiest 15 percent of the United States would own all the remaining orange properties and all properties colored purple, light blue, and dark blue. The least wealthy 80 percent of the population would then own only the four railroads and the two utilities. Critics of markets ask then how many citizens would judge the economy to be just when 20 percent of the population owns 80 percent of the wealth. While almost no critics of markets call for an absolute equality in the distribution of wealth or income, many point out that the vast majority of Americans, once informed, would object to the existing degree of inequalities as unjust.

More radical critics of markets and capitalism generally have gone on to argue that less radical critics are naïve in their belief that they can endorse a general market structure based on private ownership of productive resources while at the same time addressing the problems of distribution through taxation and other methods to redistribute prosperity to those who lose out in the process. The argument is that there is an essential cultural effect of structuring production based on private ownership and self-interest: Once production is finished, the society comes to interpret efforts at redistribution as a violation of fundamental societal norms embodied in the individualistic rules for property ownership.[19] These more radical critics insist that justice can occur only when individuals can no longer own and control our factories and other large production sites.

2. Markets Threaten the Environment

Many complaints against self-interest in markets have been lodged based on the detrimental impact of market outcomes on the environment. As even market proponents admit, individual self-interested activity will tend to ignore damaging effects of "negative externalities," detrimental effects for others that lie outside the immediate activity

---

[19] Ismael Garcia, *Justice in Latin American Theology of Liberation* (Atlanta: John Knox Press, 1987), 144.

of the individual and that the individual does not have to take into account.

Problems in this arena are well known. Atmospheric warming[20] and depletion of the ozone layer[21] are among the two most pressing global issues, but the list of real concerns is far longer and includes waste treatment and storage,[22] depletion of water[23] or petroleum,[24] and loss of habitat and consequent loss of animal and plant species.[25] Markets threaten the environment.

3. Markets Need Enforcement of Basic Justice

One of the traditional defenses of self-interest and markets has been that moralists and other critics of markets generally have been unrealistic in what they expect of an economic system. More than one religiously based endorsement of "democratic capitalism" has chided religious people for wanting to regulate the economy based on the highest values of Christian faith.[26]

Critics of self-interest and "free" markets, however, argue that it is not the highest moral values – whether religious or secular – that ought to be expected in the economy, but rather the most basic ones, those

[20] See, for example, Sydney Levitus, John I. Antonov, Timothy P. Boyer, and Cathy Stephens, "Warming of the World Ocean," *Science* 287 (March 24, 2002): 225–9; Thomas R. Karl, Neville Nicholls, and Jonathan Gregory, "The Coming Climate," *Scientific American* 276 (May, 1997): 79–83; James Hansen, "Defusing the Global Warming Time Bomb," *Scientific American* 290 (March 2004): 69–77; Paul R. Epstein, "Is Global Warming Harmful to Health?" *Scientific American* 283 (August 2000): 50–7.

[21] See, for example, "Ozone Depletion: When Less Is Not Enough," Chapter 5 of Joseph A. Davis, *Reporting on Climate Change: Understanding the Science*, second edition (Washington, D.C.: Environmental Health Center, National Safety Council, June, 2000).

[22] See, for example, William C. Blackman Jr., *Basic Hazardous Waste Management* (Boca Roton, Fla.: Lewis Publishers, 1993).

[23] See, for example, John Balbus, "Water Quality and Water Resources," in Michael McCally, ed., *Life Support: The Environment and Human Health* (Cambridge: MIT Press, 2002), 39–63.

[24] More than fifty oil-producing nations, including the United States, have passed their peak year of oil production. Global oil production will hit its peak year in the next decade, or, with the more optimistic forecasts, by 2020. With rising global demand, prices will rise significantly. See the findings of the Oil Depletion Analysis Centre (www.odac-info.org) and the Association of the Study of Peak Oil and Gas (www.asponews.org).

[25] See, for example, L. Morris Gosling and William J. Southerland, eds., *Behaviour and Conservation* (Cambridge: Cambridge University Press, 2000).

[26] Lay Commission, *The Lay Letter*, 22.

most people might agree with regardless of their personal religious or moral positions. That is, the requirements of justice in economic life should not be confused with "higher" values that some individuals or groups may hold out of personal or communal convictions. Consider an example.

Bill might not steal a valuable item that was inadvertently left out in the open, even if he judges that no one could ever trace the theft to him. He does this out of a sense of justice – that he should not take what is not his. And he might not fire an alcoholic employee out of a conviction that just treatment requires the firm to first try to help the employee deal with the alcoholism. On the other hand, when he buys a television, Bill may choose one that is simpler and less expensive than the one he would most like to have and could very well afford. His own view of the good life may lead him to live more simply and to send the money he saves to a charitable organization to help the poor. Bill sees this as an issue of economic morality, but not one of justice: He is not obliged in justice to buy this TV but is convinced of the rightness of doing so.

Others might disagree with Bill's judgment in any of these cases, but nearly everyone understands the difference between what we are obliged to do in justice and what we choose to do out of other fundamental moral considerations.

4. Market Outcomes Are Not Deserved

Critics of markets also object to the argument of market proponents that in some simple sense markets "give people what they deserve." Michael Walzer objects to this phrasing as a surreptitious vacating of the meaning of the word "deserve" in service to market ideology.[27] Walzer provides the example of a writer whose novel is at first received very poorly and who thus makes no money on the endeavor. Then, by chance, a decade later the novel is rediscovered and it is a great hit, so much so that the author becomes wealthy. To sustain the simple argument that "the market gives people what they deserve," we would have to believe that the novelist deserved nothing when the work was first published but then deserved a great deal more ten years

---

[27] Michael Walzer, *Spheres of Justice: A Defense of Pluralism and Equality* (New York: Basic Books, 1983), 108–9.

later. Surely, Walzer argues, this is not what we mean by the notion of "desert." Rather it is more accurate to say that the market simply gives people what they get. To claim that people not only get what they get but that they deserve it as well should add some conceptual element to the getting, which is absent in the case of the market. Consider a second example.

We can understand what it means when we say that the better football team lost to a weaker team as a result of two remarkable "lucky breaks" for the winners. The better team lost even though they "deserved to win." It is of course true that, having followed the rules of the game, the weaker team did in fact win fair and square and thus some might say the weaker team did in one sense "deserve" the win. But here that simply means they followed rules and won the game – no more, no less. The quite reasonable possibility that "the better team deserved to win but didn't" is based on the idea that desert requires criteria of performance. Although strong performance usually eventuates in winning, we can't detect strong performance simply by learning who won and who lost. There needs to be an independent standard of desert separate from winning, and, for the market, there would need to be an independent standard for what is "deserving" market behavior separate from whether or not someone made money in the process.

But as Lester Thurow has argued, if you look back in history to the beginnings of the great fortunes of various industries, whether that is John D. Rockefeller in oil or Ray Kroc, founder of McDonald's, at the beginning each had competitors who worked as hard and had ideas that were not distinguishably inferior to those that ultimately proved successful in the market. The point is that if one cannot tell ahead of time which of two rivals is doing the "right" things, then one person's greater success ought not be named as something that is "deserved."[28]

Charles Lindblom adds that none of the great fortunes could have been made in the first place – whether that of Henry Ford or Bill Gates – had society, and often particularly government, not prepared the way. The automobile industry would not have existed without massive road

[28] Lester C. Thurow, *The Zero-Sum Society: Distribution and the Possibilities for Economic Change* (New York: Basic Books, 1980).

building, and Microsoft would have been an empty idea in an illiterate society.[29]

On this point it is interesting to note that even the libertarian Friedrich Hayek has argued against the use of the "you get what you deserve" argument. Hayek acknowledges that it is a useful delusion to believe this, because it does lead people to get a good education and work hard at what they do. In the end, however, Hayek believes that market activity does not automatically reward desert because, however we define a "deserving" economic activity, the market may or may not reward such activity.[30]

5. Markets Should Not Be Exonerated by Blaming Culture

Critics of markets also object to the appeal to culture that proponents of markets make in deflecting accusations that the market causes problems such as greed, consumerism, the loss of values, and so on. They say that proponents use a convenient double standard in evaluating various institutions in society.

When market activity eventuates in morally objectionable outcomes – whether that is the pornography industry or the excessive debt of consumerism – proponents of markets often argue that the problem is not really with the market itself but with the broader culture and that any attempt to regulate the market by law overlooks the more basic need for the culture to address these shortcomings.

But critics note that when proponents look at other institutions they use a different standard. Market proponents often argue that public schools in our inner cities are failing, but they do not blame these failures on a weak culture of education among the families involved; rather, the schools themselves are held responsible for the failure of the children. Similarly, market proponents frequently blame on the welfare system all of the problems experienced by welfare recipients. If they were to treat this in parallel with their analysis of the market, they would instead blame the failure of the welfare system not on the system itself but on the culture of dependency that exists in

[29] Charles E. Lindblom, *The Market System: What It Is, How It Works, and What to Make of It* (New Haven, Conn.: Yale University Press, 2001), 176.
[30] Friedrich A. Hayek, *Law, Legislation and Liberty*, vol. 2, *The Mirage of Social Justice* (Chicago: University of Chicago Press, 1976), 74.

many inner-city homes and neighborhoods. And in one of the more remarkable feats of turning the tables, William McGurn seems even to attribute the illegal financial excesses at the Enron Corporation to the "find-the-loopholes ethos of our Enron's, Tyco's, WorldCom's, etc."[31] Nowhere here do we see any reference to the market incentives that rewarded handsomely, at least until the fraud was discovered, Enron's leaders.

As we have seen, one lively form of this pro-market argument has asserted that to blame the market for failures such as consumerism or venality is like blaming alcoholism on alcohol. Critics respond that the market is not the alcohol but the all-too-willing bartender who encourages the drunk to have yet another drink. More than a billion dollars a year is spent on Madison Avenue ads to shape consumers' tastes (unlike the local grocery store ad that announces prices), and it is exactly market incentives that push firms to spend this money.

Critics of markets object to praising markets for their "cultivation" of such noble virtues as honesty, hard work, and a concern for the other, while at the same time blaming all lack of virtues on failures of the culture outside the market itself. Surely, they argue, one of the morally least attractive parts of self-interest in the market is that market forces encourage the vicious behaviors that Mr. Barton's sermon at the beginning of this chapter identified as so typical of capitalism. Why should the culture be assigned the nearly impossible task of offsetting these vivid economic incentives by moral conviction?

In addition, "blaming the culture" is often linked with a naïve understanding of the function of law. All would agree that the primary function of law concerns a sort of straightforward coercion, prohibiting certain activities because they are simply unacceptable. At the same time, Cass Sunstein has argued that there is an "expressive function" of law in that it is capable of "expressing social values" and "encouraging social norms to move in particular directions."[32] One need think only of the movement for civil rights for African Americans in the

---

[31] Rebecca M. Blank and William McGurn, *Is the Market Moral? A Dialogue on Religion, Economics and Justice* (Washington, D.C.: Brookings Institution Press, 2004), 140.

[32] Cass R. Sunstein, *Free Markets and Social Justice* (New York: Oxford University Press, 1997), 57.

United States in the last half of the twentieth century. Changes in the law about voting, eating at lunch counters, and sitting in the front of buses clearly did prohibit abusive behaviors. At the same time, however, this national legal endorsement of change had a beneficial effect in increasing the social consensus that eventually brought about a reversal of attitudes within a relatively short period of time on a historical scale. The weight and inevitability of legal change did indeed help to convince individuals and communities to change. Culture influences law, but all should admit that good law improves the culture, and the economy.

6. Markets Encourage Greed

Perhaps the most fundamental problem facing those who would launch a moral defense of self-interest in markets is the long tradition of skepticism toward commercial greed that has existed in Western culture.

Twenty-three hundred years ago, Aristotle argued that the acquisition of wealth must be done properly or it will undermine both the quality of personal relationships (friendship) and the fundamentally social nature of the human person (which is fulfilled only in the public life of the citizen). For Aristotle, the idea was to reduce anxiety about the acquisition of things needed in one's household. However, he argued, "we see the opposite happening; and all who are engaged in acquisition increase their fund of currency without any limit or pause."[33] This same aversion to the risks presented by commercial greed is represented in medieval Christendom in the work of Thomas Aquinas, who argued that there is something morally dangerous about commerce and the life of the merchant, because there is no internal limit that says when to stop gaining more money.[34] As with Aristotle, the problem here is twofold. On the one hand, the individual gets drawn ever more deeply into an unending quest for more financial security, and on the other this attitude undermines the responsibility of the prosperous toward those who through no fault of their own have unmet needs.

---

[33] Thomas J. Lewis, "Acquisition and Anxiety: Aristotle's Case Against the Market," *Canadian Journal of Economics* 11 (February 1978): 69–90.
[34] Thomas Aquinas, *Summa Theologiae* (New York: Blackfriars, 1964), II–II, q.77, a.4.

Those who opposed this classic suspicion of narrow self-interest in economic life have often attempted to isolate economic life from moral considerations altogether. To the extent that this suspicion has often arisen out of a Christian point of view in Western culture, the defense has been that religion is a different realm from that of business life. Here the argument has been that different sets of standards are needed because religion is "impractical" in its endorsement of extreme self-sacrifice.

But critics of this defense of markets and self-interest argue that it is short-sighted and historically unrealistic. Markets depend heavily on the existence of moral standards such as honesty and trust. Laws to prevent dishonesty and fraud exist to prevent abuses, but the legal system would be overwhelmed if the vast majority didn't voluntarily refrain from such activities out of personal conviction. Thus a moral condemnation of greed encouraged by the market is necessary on the grounds of both moral standards and economic efficiency.

An additional argument that markets encourage greed is presented by Albert Hirschman in his analysis of the shift toward consequentialist thinking, particularly in utilitarianism, so that rationality comes to be associated with "the careful estimation of costs and benefits, with most weight necessarily being given to those that are better known and more quantifiable." Because "each person is best informed about his or her own desires, satisfactions, disappointments, and sufferings," it is a short distance to realize that this sort of view of market rationality overemphasizes effects in one's own life and undervalues those less easily quantifiable effects in the lives of others.[35]

7. Markets Undermine Culture and Their Own Moral Foundations

More than a century ago, the economist Thorstein Veblen argued that business enterprise would itself naturally decay because of two factors. The first was that the instinct of the businessman is to make a profit, whether or not this eventuates in the production of useful goods and services. The second was that "the machine discipline" of modern industry slowly undermines the "institutional heritage" on which the respect for law and order and other moral characteristics essential to

---

[35] Hirschman, *Rhetoric*, 36.

business enterprise are founded.[36] The economist Joseph Schumpeter also argued for an inevitable transformation of capitalism caused by its own internal logic.[37] Stefano Zamagni has argued that markets themselves "slowly but inexorably" undermine both norms and social conventions necessary for responsible economic life.[38] This is what Albert Hirschman has called the "self-destruction thesis" concerning capitalism.[39]

Critics of market excess argue that not only do markets undermine their own moral foundations, but they also eat away at the foundations of the rest of life. As David Hollenbach has put it, "a consumer society is one in which the spirit of the marketplace has leached into the sphere of politics, culture, and religion."[40] Even the *Wall Street Journal*'s chief editorial writer, William McGurn, has argued that "there will ever be a need to check [the market's] tendency to extend its writ beyond the realm of things useful to human beings and start applying it to human beings themselves."[41] Defenders of the market have often claimed that it encourages initiative, creativity, and invention, but critics argue that a darker experience is found on the other side of this coin. Markets lead people to think of all the areas of their lives in terms of self-interest, something that undermines the internal logic of these other areas of life.

The social philosopher Michael Walzer has argued that justice itself cannot be based on a simple one-size-fits-all understanding of what just behavior entails. In his book *Spheres of Justice*, he argues that different kinds of "goods" (i.e., things people value) have different social meanings and that the proper rule for just distribution of those goods

---

[36] Thorstein Veblen, *The Theory of Business Enterprise* (1902): (New York: New American Library, 1932). See especially Chapter 10, "The Natural Decay of Business Enterprise."

[37] Joseph Schumpeter, "The Instability of Capitalism," *Economic Journal* 38 (September 1928): 361–86.

[38] Stefano Zamagni, "Hacía una Economía Civil," *Criterio* (Buenos Aires) 70 (October 16, 1997): 24–8.

[39] Hirschman, *Rhetoric*, 110.

[40] David Hollenbach, "Christian Social Ethics After the Cold War," in *John Paul II and Moral Theology*. Readings in Moral Theology, no. 10. Charles E. Curran and Richard A. McCormick, eds. (New York: Paulist Press, 1998), 352–75. Reprinted from *Theological Studies* 53 (1992): 93.

[41] Blank and McGurn, *Is the Market Moral?*, 69–70.

depends on their meanings. Thus, for example, simple economic commodities are distributed by the rule of the market: Each will receive
as income what others are willing to offer to get the things he originally owned. But other social goods must be distributed by other rules.
Honors should go to those who deserve them, not to those who can
pay the most for them. Even though the criteria for deserving a Nobel
prize in physics are quite different from those for a gold medal in the
hundred-meter dash at the Olympics, it would be unjust to buy (or
sell) either honor. Essential goods or services, whether that is the help
of the police when one has been robbed or sufficient food to feed
one's family when one is unemployed, should be distributed in accord
with needs. Offices (jobs that have a political import of some kind)
are distributed in accord with the criteria that define them. Similarly,
citizenship, education, love, and political power are all distributed by
different principles.

Walzer's point is that different kinds of goods ought to be distributed under different rules because their diverse meanings should
be respected. Thus one of Walzer's fundamental critiques is directed
at libertarians and a number of other market proponents who see no
problem in extending the logic of the market – one person makes an
offer and the other decides whether or not to accept it – into other
areas of life where this market mentality undermines widely accepted
views of justice. From this perspective, whether or not economic self-
interest in the sphere of money and commodities is morally attractive,
it is morally quite offensive as it pushes into other spheres of life.

Critics have yet another response to the argument of market proponents that one should blame a faulty culture for many of the problems
often attributed to the market. They argue that the very institutions of
culture have become sources of market profits far more dramatically
than has ever been the case before. Television, movies, and music of
all kinds are now subject to the profit-maximizing logic of the market.
Thus, they argue, it is far more true that the market undermines culture than that the culture undermines the market.

8. Conservatives Exaggerate the Problems Created by Government
Progressives endorse Albert Hirschman's critique of the "rhetoric
of reaction." Conservatives and reactionaries have a long history of

opposition to government activity based on three exaggerated claims, or "theses."[42] The futility thesis claims that efforts at social transformation are doomed to fail. The perversity thesis claims that government efforts to counteract a problem inevitably make the problem worse. The jeopardy thesis argues that the cost of addressing problems is too high as it endangers other values important to society.

Hirschman's point is not that such things never occur – of course they do. The point is that it is false to claim they always or even usually do – and a further problem is that these three exaggerations have a long history of reoccurrence. Those opposed to government efforts to solve problems have been saying these things for centuries.

To take but a single American example, consider the Social Security program. There are debates today about how and where to invest the funds generated by the Social Security tax, but the vast majority on both left and right endorse the program. When it was being debated in Congress in 1935, opponents of the change resorted to the classic forms of Hirschman's "Rhetoric of Reaction." For example, Republican Representative James W. Wadsworth of New York argued that

this bill opens the door and invites the entrance into the political field of power so vast, so powerful as to threaten the integrity of our institutions and to pull the pillars of the temple down upon the heads of our descendants.[43]

Government regulation of market excesses is far more successful than conservative rhetoric indicates.

Conclusion

We have seen in this chapter the complexities that surround the very notion of self-interest, separate from its exercise within markets. We also reviewed a number of arguments that critics of self-interest and markets often make in their efforts to resist "free" markets endorsed by their political opponents.

---

[42] Albert O. Hirschman, *Rhetoric*, ix–x.

[43] Arthur J. Altmeyer, *The Formative Years of Social Security* (Madison: University of Wisconsin Press, 1968), 38.

Having seen in Chapter 3 the moral arguments in favor of self-interest in markets and here in Chapter 4 those against, we need to investigate one more set of issues before turning to a framework for better understanding debates over the morality of markets. We need next to consider the problems that markets, or any other form of economic organization, need to address.

5

The Four Problems of Economic Life

One way to understand the strengths and weaknesses of markets is to ask, "What should an economy do?" Many of the differences in the evaluation of markets can be traced to differences in emphasis in the kind of problems that the proponents and critics of markets believe an economic system must address.

In a classic essay from the 1920s,[1] Frank H. Knight outlined five problems that any economy must address. For our purposes they can be grouped into two categories. The first category – including problems one, two, four, and five in Knight's list – concerns what is to be produced, how it is to be produced, how much of production goes to immediate consumption and how much to investment, and how to adjust consumption when production in the short run is greater or less than usual. These are the issues where the discipline of economics has historically felt most at home. Thus, one quite standard definition of economics in the introductory textbooks is as follows:

Economics is the study of how individuals, experiencing virtually limitless wants, choose to allocate scarce resources to best satisfy their wants.[2]

---

[1] Frank H. Knight, *The Economic Organization* (New York: Augustus M. Kelley, 1967), 3–15. Knight's essay was written in the 1920s, privately printed in 1933, and first published in 1951.
[2] Robert B. Ekelund Jr. and Robert D. Tollison, *Economics: Private Markets and Public Choice*, sixth edition (New York: Addison-Wesley, 2000), 4.

The second category, Knight's third problem to be solved, is what he calls "the function of distribution," the social determination concerning who gets what goods and services produced in the nation.[3] Although the moral issues surrounding distribution are universally noted by economists, economics itself has in general limited its work to identifying the empirical results of who gets what without entering into the more fundamental question "Who *should* get what?"

Knight's typology is helpful, but it omits two other issues essential to economic life. The first concerns global environmental problems. While a few farsighted scholars of Knight's day noted such issues, the vast majority of scientists and policy makers at the time – whether from right or left, whether in economics or other disciplines – were largely unaware of the long-term problems of environmental degradation that became so vivid by the end of the twentieth century.

The second oversight in Knight's typology concerns the role of human relations in the economy, and the moral and legal embodiment of values that undergird and make possible even the most elementary forms of economic cooperation. These concerns have been long identified by humanists (often as part of a critique of markets), but recent work within economics has brought such issues within the purview of economic analysis as well.

Thus, in our description of the problems of economic life that markets must address, we will identify four separate issues. Following the vast majority of mainstream economists, the first two will be the *allocation* of scarce resources to alternative uses and the *distribution* of the goods and services to the various persons in society. A third issue will be that of the *scale* of the economy, a shorthand way of acknowledging that a continually growing economy must eventually bump up against the limits of a planetary biosphere of fixed size, causing macro-level problems that individual self-interested economic actors have little incentive to address. The fourth problem is the *quality of human relations*. The smooth functioning of economic life, even on a high-tech factory floor, is possible only if there is a pattern of predictable, and largely moral, relationships among the persons involved. In economic

[3] For another, quite similar analysis of the "five basic decisions of economic organization," see Henry N. Sanborn, *What, How, for Whom: The Decisions of Economic Organization* (Baltimore: Cotter-Barnard Company, 1972), 3.

jargon, this has been analyzed as an issue of "social capital." This chapter briefly examines each of the four problems.

A fifth important problem needs to be identified, but its character is different from that of the others: It cuts across all four problems as a dimension of each. This problem is *reproduction*, the necessity of investing resources simply to maintain the capacity one already possesses.[4] Businesses know well the need to replace machines and other physical capital as they wear out with use, and for this reason they regularly set aside funds for depreciation. Without this ongoing reinvestment, existing capital equipment would continue to produce until it was worn out, at which point the business would be at a great loss if it had not made plans for its replacement. Thus, reproduction is an essential dimension of the problem of allocation just identified. But it is an equally important dimension of the other three problems, as we shall see. Environmentally, of course, sustainability is a matter of attending to the ongoing capacity of the natural world to maintain processes we have come to depend on. Interestingly, even the questions of distribution and the quality of human relations have an essential dimension of reproduction to them, as we shall see.

The Four Problems of Economic Life

Before outlining these four problems of economic life in more detail, it is important to note that differences between proponents and critics of markets lead them to evaluate – and even describe – these four problems differently. Even the task of identifying the problems that need to be addressed – how many there are and of what sort – requires both empirical and moral discernment. Mainstream economists who prefer to think of their social science as "value free" stress the empirical conspicuousness of the two problems that Knight identifies. But the best of the discipline acknowledge that, in economics as in every science, the decision to investigate some issues and not others always entails a process of valuing that goes beyond empirical analysis.[5] To help sort out these differences, each of the four problems will be described

---

4 I am indebted to Barbara Hilkert Andolson for suggesting this line of analysis.
5 For a description, see Daniel M. Hausman, "Introduction," in *The Philosophy of Economics: An Anthology*, second edition (New York: Cambridge University Press, 1994).

primarily from the point of view of those who emphasize this particular problem in conversations about the strengths or weaknesses of markets.

To accomplish this analysis, the chapter first examines each of the four problems separately, identifying the strengths and weaknesses of markets in addressing that issue. Then it examines the negative interdependence among the four problems – how improving one can exacerbate another. Finally, it examines the positive interdependence – how making progress on one problem can assist in addressing another. Table 5-1 summarizes the characteristics of each problem. Two other tables are provided later to summarize the interrelationships.

1. Allocation

The first of the four problems to be faced in any economy is that of allocation. The problem itself is an old one in economics, but applying the word "allocation" to market processes (and not simply to government decision) is a twentieth-century phenomenon. The goal and predominant value implicit here is the production of wealth, the goods and services that people find beneficial. Economists today understand the problem as one of the allocation of resources principally because of a shift in the self-understanding of the discipline.[6] Mainstream economics now understands itself primarily as the study of the allocation of scarce (and, therefore, costly) resources to alternative uses.

Those who have stressed production as the preeminent problem of economic life have also typically stressed the role of individual consumers as the ones who decide what should be produced, extolling "consumer sovereignty" based on individuals' decisions to spend their money on one product rather than on another. Markets then are seen ultimately as servants of the freedom and self-interest of individual market actors. As Charles Lindblom has put it, the market provides coordination without a coordinator.[7]

---

[6] The economist Lionel Robbins is a key figure in this transition because of his broadening of economic science from the study of wealth production to the study of human choice under conditions of scarcity, where each economic agent must allocate scarce resources to accomplish competitive ends. See Lionel Robbins, *An Essay on the Nature and Significance of Economic Science* (London: Macmillan, 1946).

[7] Charles E. Lindblom, *The Market System: What It Is, How It Works, and What to Make of It* (New Haven, Conn.: Yale University Press, 2001), 23.

TABLE 5-1. *The Four Problems of Economic Life*

Problem	General Goal	Predominant Values of Advocates	Primary Perceived Evils	Primary Locus of Decisions	Major Goal in Current Context	Effects of the Need for Reproduction
Allocation	Production	Wealth creation, efficiency, freedom, self-interest	Waste and inefficiency, government interference, monopoly	Market	Increase efficiency	Renewal of physical and human capital
Distribution	Equity	Property rights; economic rights; meeting needs; rewarding effort, risk, and sacrifice	Poverty, concentrated wealth, bad incentive structures, self-interest, big government	Government and nonprofit organizations	Reduce inequality	Periodic renegotiation of public standards of equity
Scale	Sustainability	Conservation, recycling, limits to growth, appropriate technology	Unsustainable growth, discounting the future	Government and international agreements	Ecological viability, controlled growth	Regulation of threats to the Earth's carrying capacity
Quality of relations	Strong persons in active communities	Individuality; community/ participation; culture/tradition; democracy, freedom, and responsibility	Loss of individuality, loss of community	Local, regional, and national communities	Community standards, responsive bureaucracy	Renewal of social and organizational capital

The primary evil confronting efforts at production is waste and inefficiency. These can occur in the production process, as when more resources than necessary are used to produce something. It can also occur at the point of the marketing of products, as when there is an oversupply of a particular good at prices that will cover its costs of production, from which we learn that some of those resources should instead have been used to produce other goods in shorter supply. This understanding of the importance of waste in the process is the point at which the notion of efficiency enters the discussion. No one is in favor of inefficiency. Everyone – from profit-seeking entrepreneurs to nature-loving environmentalists – wants resources to stretch as far as possible.

The primary locus of decision making about allocation is the market. Typically, individuals and private institutions own most resources, and the market is "the place" where owners make decisions about what to do with them. These individual decisions are always limited by technological possibilities of the era and, as we will see more clearly in Chapter 7, they are constrained by cultural, moral, and governmental standards.

The primary method by which governments influence persons making market decisions is to offer incentives (e.g., government contracts to produce roads, or tax breaks for firms that purchase new equipment) or to impose disincentives (e.g., taxes to reduce cigarette smoking, or prison sentences to discourage drug trafficking). There is a constant danger that individuals or institutions will react to these new "signals" from government in ways not foreseen by the legislators who created them. For example, consider the standard economic argument against rent controls or gasoline price ceilings. Although people who *can find* apartments to rent or gasoline to buy will be helped, builders of apartments and refiners of gasoline will reduce or even cease production of these products if they cannot cover their costs. As a result, fewer people will be *able to find* them for lease or sale. Similarly, without competition in the market, monopoly (one seller), cartels (collusion among sellers), or monopsony (one buyer) would distort efficient allocation because persons or organizations with such "market power" will employ that power to their own advantage and to the detriment of others'. Anti-trust laws exist to prevent such abuses.

Reproduction as a problem cuts across the problem of allocation because of the simple fact that the capacity to produce goods and services must itself be reproduced or it will be depleted. Firms set aside funds for capital depreciation, and homeowners periodically do house repairs in order to maintain the structure's capacity to provide shelter. But reproduction raises other issues as well, as feminist economists and social theorists have argued cogently in recent decades.[8] Even something as basic as the supply of workers from one generation to the next requires an immense investment of human effort and energy, largely done by women and mostly ignored in the history of economic analysis. Children must be borne, nurtured, socialized, and educated before they can become productive members of any economic system. Feminists have criticized the short-sightedness of the economic presumption of self-interest because this absolutely essential task of reproduction has historically depended largely on one-half of the human race, women, who have often had to set aside their own interests, economic and otherwise, in the rearing of their children.[9]

Nonetheless, the problem of allocation, especially as described by those who emphasize its preeminence, prominently features the self-interest of economic actors. As we saw in Chapter 2, it was a preoccupation with allocation that allowed Milton Friedman, James Buchanan, and Friedrich Hayek to believe that the market system could be justified without recourse to moral concerns beyond self-interest. And as we saw in Chapter 3, advocates of free markets also combine this feature with an advocacy of personal freedom as a value in itself, something that falls under problem four, the quality of relations. This is not an insignificant issue in a world where the people of some nations might lead healthier and more prosperous lives if more economic decisions were left to the local level. Still, compared with the other three problems, allocation is preeminently dependent on active, free persons and institutions' making decisions largely out of self-interest.

---

[8] See, for example, Diana Strassmann, "Feminist Economics," in Janice Peterson and Margaret Lewis, eds., *The Elgar Companion to Feminist Economics* (Cheltenham: Edward Elgar, 1999), 360–73.

[9] See, for example, Susan Moller Okin's critique of libertarianism, *Justice, Gender, and the Family* (New York: Basic Books, 1989), 74–88.

And the primary goal of those most concerned with the problem of allocation in our current context is to increase efficiency.[10]

2. *Distribution*

The second of the four problems that must be addressed by every economic system is distribution – the distribution of the products and services available each year to individuals and organizations. When we ask *to whom* the benefits of the economy should go, we ask a question of equity, of morality, of justice. By and large, economists recognize this.

Differences in perspective on what makes for a just distribution are immense. Libertarians would stress property rights while others on the political right emphasize the importance of rewarding effort, risk, and sacrifice. Those further to the left talk about economic rights (say, to food or shelter) and meeting needs, in addition to appropriately rewarding effort, risk, and sacrifice and even achieving a fair relative income. The primary perceived evils in distribution range from concerns of the right (big government and taxation) to concerns of the left (poverty and great concentrations of wealth). Both groups criticize faulty incentive structures and the self-interest of persons who have something to gain in resisting or encouraging redistribution. Among institutionalized disincentives are welfare policies that discourage the seeking of employment, legal structures that foster costly litigiousness, and campaign finance policies under which a dollar spent by a corporation trying to change the government's rules of the game in favor of the firm can improve corporate profitability more than spending that dollar productively to increase efficiency.

The primary locus of decisions in matters of distribution – whether defined by libertarians or by Marxists – is the national community, principally the national government that sets the economic rules. Charitable, voluntary efforts are important at all levels, but the most basic need for a structure of justly distributed wealth is that embedded in the

---

[10] There is always a problem in deciding whether and by how much "wealth" changes from year to year. One usual measure is the Gross National Product (GNP), but it has many limitations as a measure for economic welfare. The treatment of allocation here ignores difficulties in any definition of what counts for "improvement," thereby leaving some quite important issues unaddressed.

national economy. The primary goal of those most concerned about distribution in our context is to reduce inequality.

The need for "reproduction" cuts across the concerns of distribution just as it did in allocation. No economic or political system can long endure in a democracy if the citizens do not have a rough confidence in the equity of the system itself. People may think that their own work is undervalued and underpaid, but personal discontent won't lead to political instability unless there is a more general sense of injustice in the distribution of wealth and income within the economic system. This sense of publicly endorsed standards of equity must itself be produced and reproduced from one generation to the next. Families, schools, and civic celebrations all contribute, and periodically there is a renegotiation of publicly accepted standards of equity.

Historical examples here include contemporary presumptions about Social Security in old age (dating in the United States from President Franklin Delano Roosevelt's New Deal) and changes in the economic and social status of African Americans in the century following the Civil War. Distribution is not simply an objective fact in an economic system but a moral issue and a subject of popular perception as well.

3. Scale

The third problem facing the modern economy is achieving the proper scale within the natural world. This is a relatively new problem. There have been examples of premodern problems of scale, but these have been localized phenomena. The cliff-dwelling Anasazi of what is now southwestern Colorado flourished for several hundred years and then disappeared in a matter of decades in the early thirteenth century, probably because they overtaxed the environment in a period of drought.[11] Similarly, citizens of the large industrial cities of England in the nineteenth century often experienced days when a miasma of fog and coal smoke filled the air and their lungs. The London *Times* reported in January 1812 that for most of the previous day, "it was impossible to read or write at a window without artificial light. Persons

---

[11] Elenor H. Ayer, *The Anasazi* (New York: Walker and Company, 1993), 60–3; William M. Ferguson, *The Anasazi of Mesa Verde and the Four Corners* (Boulder: University Press of Colorado, 1996), 99–100, 114.

in the street could scarcely be seen in the forenoon at two yards distance."[12] Still, these were exceptions. Only in the last several decades of the twentieth century did people develop an acute sense of the limits of the planetary biosphere as a storehouse for natural resources and a sink for wastes.

Problems of worldwide scale are completely beyond the reach and ken of unconstrained individual economic activity in the market. Market decisions by individuals and firms that work so well to improve allocation – quick adjustments to changing prices out of self-interest – ignore the problem of scale. For millennia, humans had a negligible impact on the Earth's ecosystems. Today the technological power that has increased the economic well-being of most people in the industrialized world has grown so large that it threatens key elements of the natural systems on which this prosperity depends. And most economic analysis has been slow to catch up.

Economists have long analyzed the efficiency problems facing owners of the right to use up oil or water resources that exist in a large common pool to which other owners also have a right. Left to individual decisions, these common pools will be depleted too quickly, in an inefficient manner, as owners decide to get as much as they can before there's none left. Efficiency can exist only with coordination, either imposed from the outside by government or established by a cooperative agreement by all the owners of rights to deplete the pool.[13] Economists have similarly noted the existence of "externalities" or "neighborhood effects." These are either negative effects of economic actions felt by others where the costs are not paid by those causing them (pollution is the classic case), or positive effects caused for others where those causing them cannot reap the benefits (as when neighbors benefit from seeing the nicely manicured lawns of the corporate headquarters in their town).

Economists have long analyzed the issue of optimal scale for a business. In the jargon of economics, each organization should expand its production to the point where its rising marginal costs exactly equal

---

[12] *The Times*, Saturday, January 11, 1812, quoted in Barbara Freese, *Coal: A Human History* (Cambridge, Mass.: Perseus Books, 2003), 27.
[13] See, for example, Elinor Ostrom, Laurie Gardner, and James Walker, *Rules, Games, and Common-Pool Resources* (Ann Arbor: University of Michigan Press), 1994.

its declining marginal benefits from expansion. Developed in an era when planetary environmental problems were largely unanticipated, economics as a discipline has rarely applied this analysis of optimal scale to the economy as a whole.

Clearly the problem of planetary scale of the economy today is not only real but also immensely important. As we saw in Chapter 4, in the critique of self-interest in markets, global warming and the depletion of the ozone layer are perhaps the two most pressing issues, but the list of real concerns is far longer: waste treatment and storage, depletion of water or petroleum, loss of habitat and consequent loss of animal and plant species, and so on. While some of these may be tractable by technological breakthrough,[14] the point here is that treating the problem of allocation as if it were far and away more important than the problem of scale is short-sighted and foolhardy. As Herman Daly and John Cobb put it in the language familiar to economists, determining the appropriate scale for the economy within the biosphere is a "distinct optimization problem," one that cannot be subsumed under the effort to achieve an allocative optimum.[15]

The general goal guiding responses to the problem of scale is sustainability. The primary perceived evil when talking of scale is mindless, unsustainable growth or what Herman Daly has called "uneconomic growth."[16] If world industrial production continues apace, serious climatic temperature shifts of even a few degrees Celsius due to global warming could impose staggering and irreversible economic costs.[17]

If the production of energy continues to require more and more energy inputs to produce the same amount of energy to be sold (and this is likely as the more accessible sources of energy are consumed first, in good, economically rational fashion), petroleum will by the

[14] For one example – how the presence of biogenic isoprene can reduce the production of nitric oxide in coal and fired power plants – see Ryerson et al., "Observation of Ozone Formation in Power Plant Plumes and Implications for Ozone Control Strategies," in *Science* 292 (April 27, 2001), 719.

[15] Herman E. Daly and John B. Cobbs Jr., *For the Common Good: Redefining Economy Toward Community, the Environment, and a Sustainable Future* (Boston: Beacon Press, 1989), 145.

[16] Herman E. Daly, "Beyond Growth: Avoiding Uneconomic Growth," in Mohan Munasinghe et al., eds., *The Sustainability of Long-Term Growth: Socio-economic and Ecological Perspectives* (Cheltenham: Edward Elgar, 2002), 153–71.

[17] Paul R. Epstein, "Is Global Warming Harmful to Health?" *Scientific American* 283 (August, 2000): 50–7; James Hensen "Defusing the Global Warming Time Bomb," *Scientific American* 290 (March 2004): 68–77.

middle of the twenty-first century recede dramatically as a significant world energy source.[18] Nuclear power from safer and cleaner fission reactors[19] and nuclear fusion[20] remain possibilities, but technological uncertainties and public attitudes remain as significant barriers to any confidence that they can replace petroleum as the world's primary energy source.

The problem of reproduction is more vividly apparent within the question of scale than in the other three problems. Many of our economic practices are not indefinitely sustainable, and finding ways to accomplish our economic goals without undermining this sustainability is the essence of finding the proper scale. The key insight, of course, is that when the "footprint" of the human economy was small in comparison with the biosphere, there was little need to worry that the human economy could reproduce itself over and over. Now that the footprint of the human economy has become so much larger – and is growing faster – in a biosphere whose size has not changed, there is simply less room to continue to replicate these economic processes. Moving from an "empty" world to a "full" world has brought the problem of reproduction to center stage.

In spite of the shortcomings of markets in the creation of the problem of scale, market-related remedies have already proven helpful in addressing environmental problems. Judicious governmental use of tax incentives and tradeable permits can serve long-term sustainability. International environmental treaties can specify standards that individual nations can meet by market-based incentive systems.

Historians of the next century may shake their heads at what today look like reasonable market decisions. In hindsight, these may appear as short-sighted choices based on a naïve extrapolation from two centuries of good fortune built on the exhaustion of a resource base of petroleum, natural gas, and underground water supplies that took a hundred thousand times that long to create. Technological breakthroughs may help, but fundamentally the problem of scale is an immense and intractable one for any modern economy.

---

[18] For an early prediction, see John Gever, Robert Kaufmann, David Skole, and Charles Vorosmarty, *Beyond Oil: The Threat to Food and Fuel in the Coming Decades* (Cambridge, Mass.: Ballinger Publishing Co., 1986), especially Chapter 2.

[19] James A. Lake, Ralph G. Bennett, and John F. Kotek, "Next Generation of Nuclear Power," *Scientific American* 286 (January 2002): 73–81.

[20] Harold P. Furth, "Fusion," *Scientific American* 273 (September 1995): 174–7.

4. The Quality of Human Relations

The fourth problem is the quality of human relations. This is the most complex of the four in that it could also be described as a panoply of related problems. Still, as our purpose in this chapter is the development of a framework for thinking generally about the economy, the constraints of space require brevity.

The governing goal of this fourth problem of the quality of relations is to develop and sustain strong persons in active communities. This problem needs to be seen as integral to economic life – and not a peripheral concern attended to only by moral or cultural realms – for two reasons. The first is that economic life generally, *as well as economic life considered narrowly as allocation,* is possible only to the extent that the individuals and communities involved are well constituted. The second is that the experience of relations among persons at one's job is one of the primary socializing influences of adults in modern culture, and this experience strongly shapes our views of what is "ordinary" or even "natural" for humans. As the economist Rebecca Blank has put it, "economic institutions also shape norms and political practices."[21]

The primary values to be achieved under the heading of the quality of relations are individuality, creativity, community, and participation. The meaning of any one of these is widely debated and heavily influenced by a nation's culture and informal traditions, but clearly within the United States these goals entail democracy, freedom, and accountability. The primary perceived evils are polar opposites: the loss of the individual in the group and the loss of community as a result of individualism. The locus for decisions concerning this vitality of persons and communities is less focused than for any of the other three problems: individuals' decisions and those taken at any level of group interaction. Actions to improve relations can range from religiously motivated individual decisions to treat co-workers better, to business decisions implementing employee training programs to improve corporate culture, to government decisions to strengthen sexual harassment laws.

Any assessment of the major goal to be accomplished in our current context will also be subject to diverse interpretations. Nonetheless, from the perspective of those most concerned with this problem, two

---

[21] Rebecca M. Blank and William McGurn, *Is the Market Moral? A Dialogue on Religion, Economics and Justice* (Washington, D.C.: Brookings Institution Press, 2004), 97.

stand out: The first is strengthening communal standards to improve the quality of relations, and the second is limiting the psychic distance that threatens human relations in large bureaucracies, whether in government, business, or nonprofit organizations. These two, of course, are themselves in tension, but together they mark the importance of responsive and robust channeling of economic activity. Note here that there are other chronic objections to bureaucracy, most notably that it can obstruct good allocation (the first problem), but it qualifies here as well in that the rigidities and unresponsiveness that so often accompany bureaucracy are detrimental to individuals and community.

Reproduction is particularly important in addressing the quality of relations. Feminist analysis has rightly stressed the importance of both equality for women in the economic sphere and the adjustments necessary in business expectations for employees who have parental responsibilities (whether mothers or fathers). As Susan Moller Okin has put it, two typical presumptions of business must change: that "women are primarily responsible for the rearing of children" and that "serious and committed members of the workforce (regardless of class) do not have primary responsibility, or even shared responsibility, for the rearing of children."[22]

Although the discipline of economics has for most of its history generally ignored these concerns about the quality of human relations, they are without doubt essential to any adequate analysis of economic productivity. Beginning with a now classic effort by Harvey Leibenstein[23] to define "X-efficiency," contemporary economic analysis has come to address the quality of relations under the rubric of "social capital."

Social capital is, of course, a metaphor. It builds on the economist's notion of "capital," which represents machines and tools that make production more efficient but that require an expenditure of time and effort to construct. This economic concept was first broadened into the analogy of "human capital," representing the skills and ability

---

[22] Okin, *Justice*, 5.
[23] Harvey Leibenstein, "Allocative Efficiency versus 'X-Efficiency,'" *American Economic Review* 56 (June 1966): 392–415. For an early example of the study of the influence of attitudes and other non-economic elements in the workplace, see F. J. Roethlisberger and William J. Dickson, *Management and the Worker* (Cambridge, Mass.: Harvard University Press, 1939).

of an individual, which took time and effort to develop, usually through formal education and training. The notion of social capital, then, is a further extension of this idea to name the character of social relationships that makes all sorts of human activities – economic, political, and social – more "productive." Thus the notion of social capital includes commonly shared moral norms like civility and mutual respect as well as relations between persons mediated by organizations such as businesses, schools, or voluntary associations.[24] An additional dimension of social capital includes broader institutions and social structures themselves; societies operate better when they have fundamental agreements about civil liberties, the rule of law, the courts and police, the structure of government, and so on. All these represent a kind of social capital that is often taken for granted when it operates well but is sorely missed when it is not present, for example in nations with severe problems of government corruption.

Social capital links economic, social, and political areas of life and improves the efficiency of economic activities through both formal and informal organizations. In economic terms it is based on the quite reasonable assumption that "desirable social relationships in institutions have positive externalities."[25] Because individuals are unable to appropriate all the benefits generated by their personal efforts to create more social capital, individual actors have a tendency to invest in less social capital than would be economically efficient.[26] For this reason those responsible for the commonweal – whether corporate managers overseeing the firm, or democratically elected government representatives – have an economic rationale for public subsidy in the creation of social capital.[27]

---

[24] For a discussion of "organizational capital," see John Tomer, *Organizational Capital: The Path to Higher Productivity and Well-being* (New York: Praeger Publishing Co., 1987).

[25] Ismail Serageldin and Christiaan Grootaert, *Defining Social Capital: An Integrating View* (Washington, D.C.: World Bank, 1997), 47.

[26] Ironically, it is also true that the more social capital there is in a society, the more efficient is the creation of human capital by individuals in education and training. See, for example, James S. Coleman, "Social Capital in the Creation of Human Capital," *American Journal of Sociology* 94 (Supplement: Organizations and Institutions: Sociological and Economic Approaches to Analysis of Social Structure, 1988): S109.

[27] World Bank analysis of the various forms of "capital" has developed rough calculations that only 16 to 20 percent of the wealth of 192 countries in the study consisted in human-made capital. Social capital and human capital (education and training of persons) exceed the value of all natural and human-produced assets combined,

In sum, economists and other researchers are slowly coming around to the awareness that how people relate to one another – both as individuals and as mediated by institutions – is an important economic problem.

Negative Interactions Among Efforts to Address the Four Problems

Having briefly outlined the character of the four problems facing every economy, it is helpful to note the interactions among the four, as efforts to solve one problem produce both positive and negative effects on the others. In this section, and represented in outline form in Table 5-2 (reading across each row from left to right), is a brief summary of the negative interactions between the efforts to solve the various problems. The following section addresses the positive interactions.

Allocation can be impaired by efforts to improve distribution through a loss of incentive on the part of those benefiting from government transfers[28] (whether payments to the unemployed or tax breaks for big business) or through a drop of savings and investment when taxes on incomes are raised to pay for other redistributive measures.[29] The sort of controls needed to address the problem of scale can easily lead to special-interest distortions (where small groups with a

---

except in a few nations that are heavy exporters of raw material. *Monitoring Environmental Progress – A Report on Work in Progress* (Washington, D.C.: World Bank, 1995), cited in Serageldin and Grootaert, 42.

[28] See Sheldon Danziger, Robert Haveman, and Robert Plotnick, "How Income Transfer Programs Affect Work, Saving and the Income Distribution: A Critical Review," in *Journal of Economic Literature* 19 (September 1981): 216–22. See also Nicholas Barr, "Economic Theory and the Welfare State: A Survey and Interpretation," in *Journal of Economic Literature* 30 (June 1992): 741–803.

[29] Of course, simply crying wolf here is no proof that the wolf is near. In spite of Reagan-era assertions that tax reductions for the wealthy would be the key to investment and an end to the major recession of the early 1980s, most economists now agree that consumer spending (and not a rise in tax-induced investment) brought the end to the recession, a very Keynesian solution and not a supply-side one. See Peter Lindert, *Growing Public: Social Spending and Economic Growth Since the Eighteenth Century*, two volumes (New York: Cambridge University Press, 2004). See also Nicholas Barr, "Economic Theory and the Welfare State: A Survey and Interpretation," in *Journal of Economic Literature* 30 (June 1992): 741–803; Robert Moffitt, "Incentive Effects of the U.S. Welfare System: A Review," in *Journal of Economic Literature* 30 (March 1992): 1–61.

TABLE 5-2. *Threats Arising from Goals Related to:*

	Allocation	Distribution	Scale	Quality of Relations
Allocation		Loss of incentive, drop in savings/investment	Special-interest distortions, bureaucratic blunders	Increased costs in production, special-interest distortions
Distribution	Equitable distribution is ignored by the market		Reductions in scale and in wealth make redistribution harder; special-interest distortions	Higher costs and lower wealth make redistribution harder
Scale	Markets don't internalize social costs	Redistribution is easier with growth		Higher costs and lower wealth make it harder to impose environmental limits
Quality of relations	The market undercuts communal ties and values	Mindless redistribution erodes individuality, families, customs, and values	Heavy authority in national community erodes freedom	

lot to gain will spend a lot to influence regulation) and bureaucratic blunders harmful to allocation. Efforts to sustain and improve the quality of relations in economic life often have significant costs (e.g., court systems to enforce contracts, education on the dangers of drugs or smoking, due process requirements within firms, etc.); and special-interest distortions are always possible as individuals and groups seek gains for themselves under the banner of improving the quality of relations generally.

Turning to distribution, it is clear that actions oriented to improving allocation often have effects at odds with the goals of distribution. Some bases for desert – need, for example – are entirely ineffective within the market. Other bases for desert – like effort or risk – are often rewarded by the market, but only the most doctrinaire free marketeers or libertarians would assert that this is the morally optimal scheme for rewarding effort and risk. Goals related to the problem of scale can likewise threaten distribution, as when special-interest effects (always oriented to the powerful, not the poor) or environmentally necessary economic retrenchments leave fewer resources available for redistributive efforts. Similarly, efforts to improve the quality of relations would impair distributive efforts if higher costs of achieving better relations diminished wealth, making redistribution harder, either economically or politically.[30]

Efforts to solve the problem of scale are threatened by actions in service to allocation in that individuals and institutions have market incentives to ignore the social costs they cause (pollution, of course, is the classic case).[31] And because improvements in both distribution

---

[30] Ironically, some well-founded programs designed to bring the poor out of poverty can actually increase the inequality of wealth across the nation. Social Security is a case in point. While the benefits have greatly helped the elderly, reducing poverty dramatically among retired citizens, the fact that the Social Security tax has an income cap (about \$90,000 in 2005) means that those making more than that pay a smaller share of their income in Social Security taxes than those whose income falls below the cap. See Jagadeesh Gokhale and Lawrence J. Kotlikoff, "The Impact of Social Security and Other Factors on the Distribution of Wealth," Chapter 3, in Martin Feldstein and Jeffrey B Liebman, eds., *The Distributional Aspects of Social Security and Social Security Reform* (Chicago: University of Chicago Press, 2002), 114.

[31] For an interesting review of possibilities for developing countries to avoid the environmental mistakes of the more developed nations, see Mohan Munasinghe, "Is Environmental Degradation an Inevitable Consequence of Economic Growth? Tunneling Through the Environmental Kuznets Curve," in *Ecological Economics* 29 (1999): 89–109.

and the quality of relations are generally costly, and thus easier with economic growth, efforts to address these problems will often conflict with simultaneous efforts to confront the problem of scale, which is exaggerated as the economy grows.[32]

Similarly, efforts to improve the quality of relations are threatened by the goals related to the other problems. The tendency for the market to undercut communal ties and traditional values has been well documented and criticized. Some, such as Schumpeter[33] and Veblen,[34] have even argued that this tendency in capitalism erodes the moral foundations on which capitalism must stand, thereby leading to the demise of capitalism itself. Similarly, some attempts to improve distribution (e.g., welfare rules that refuse benefits to two-parent families) may erode family ties, individuality, customs, and the like.[35] And the strong national and international authorities needed to address the problem of scale could generate restrictions on democratic freedoms.[36]

Positive Interactions Among Efforts to Address the Four Problems

At the same time, of course, solutions to these four problems are not mutually exclusive. Carefully conceived and implemented, efforts to address one problem can have positive effects on the others, as Table 5-3 summarizes briefly.

The most important of these positive interactions are those between allocation and the other three problems.

Efforts to improve distribution can indeed conduce to greater productivity. Without a broadly accepted conception of equity in a society,

[32] For one review of the relation between population and environmental problems, see Renata Serra, "The Causes of Environmental Degradation: Population, Scarcity and Growth," Chapter 4 of Timothy Swanson, ed., *The Economics of Environmental Degradation: Tragedy of the Commons?* (Cheltenham: Edward Elgar, 1996).

[33] Joseph A. Schumpeter, *Capitalism, Socialism and Democracy* (New York: Harper, 1942).

[34] Thorstein Veblen, *The Theory of Business Enterprise* (New York: New American Library, 1958). See especially Chapter 10, "The Natural Decay of Business Enterprise."

[35] Some research has indicated that efforts to increase the labor supply of single mothers in welfare programs may be based on a misdiagnosis of the problem, as "labor supply and earnings among female heads are not abnormally low, at least compared with those of married women." See Robert Moffitt, "Incentive Effects of the U.S. Welfare System: A Review," in *Journal of Economic Literature* 30 (March 1992): 57.

[36] For an early prediction of this sort of problem, see Robert Heilbroner, *An Inquiry into the Human Prospect* (New York: Norton, 1974).

TABLE 5-3. *Support Arising from Goals Related to:*

	Allocation	Distribution	Scale	Quality of Relations
Allocation		A sense of equity generates greater loyalty and motivation	Sustainable methods prevent problems that will slow future growth	Better relations increase motivation and creativity
Distribution	Redistribution is easier with greater wealth		Sustainability makes long-run equity more possible	Better relations increase interest in greater equity
Scale	Greater wealth makes environmental restrictions more affordable	Greater equity generates greater willingness to sacrifice for sustainability		Better relations generate greater willingness to sacrifice for sustainability
Quality of relations	Greater wealth makes improvements more affordable, creativity and individuality rewarded	Greater equity improves the quality of relations	Sustainability means fewer environmental losers and prevents dislocation from social crises	

both workplace predictability and political stability are at risk. Efforts to improve distribution affect workplace loyalty and motivation and enable lower-income citizens to become better educated and thereby better able to advance economically through productive contributions to the economy.[37]

Steps to address scale are also crucial for allocation. Without attention to a sustainable economic process, rapid economic growth today may well produce severe costs in the future and will look short-sighted, even foolhardy, fifty years from now. When intergenerational equity is taken into consideration (and there are few morally weighty arguments for discounting the welfare of future generations the way self-interest in the market tends to), sustainability moves from a prudent reasonableness to a moral obligation.

As important as the goals of equity and sustainability are for allocation, the goal of developing strong individuals and communities is even more critical. Neo-conservative defenders of the market system often praise the productive, wealth-producing capacity of capitalism as the engine providing the means for accomplishing other goals in life like equity or environmental improvements. However, it is just as accurate to say that it is the presence of strong, creative, and public-spirited individuals in strong, creative, and caring communities and institutions that have made possible the dramatic advances in productivity within the market system.[38] The arguments of Schumpeter and Veblen and others are telling when they point out that the rationality of the market (a "means–end" rationality) tends to undercut the values and communal ties without which the freedom and individuality that fuel the market will burn too hot and consume the very network of relationships that supports the interrelated productive centers we call the economy.[39]

---

[37] For a study of how efforts to increase equity can assist in improving efficiency, see Rebecca M. Blank, "Can Equity and Efficiency Complement Each Other?", conference paper available at http://www.fordschool.umich.edu/research/papers/PDFfiles/02–001.pdf.

[38] For one relevant analysis, see Walter J.S. Schultz, *The Moral Conditions of Economic Efficiency* (Cambridge: Cambridge University Press, 2001). For one analysis of the negative effects of sexual harassment on the efficiency of an organization, see "Sexual Harassment in the Federal Workplace: Trends, Progress, Continuing Challenges," *A Report to the President and the Congress of the United States* (U.S. Merit Systems Protection Board, Washington D.C., 1997).

[39] For the study for the importance of nonmonetary rewards and interpersonal relations on both workers' satisfaction and job efficiency, see Carlo Borzaga and Sara

While the positive interaction among the other permutations of these four problems is important, they are both less intricate and less controverted. Improving distribution is easier, other things being equal, with economic growth. While many efforts to improve sustainability compete for real resources with efforts to improve distribution, it is clear that long-run improvements in distribution require sustainable long-term economic prosperity. Similarly, with the improvement of the vitality of individuals and communities comes a greater appreciation of the value of equity within the nation.

The goals related to the problem of scale clearly conflict with the unencumbered operation of the market, but it is also true that environmentally necessary changes in production will be easier to make with rising national wealth, particularly the more that economic growth is an environmentally benign sort. Advances in equity will likely bring about a greater willingness to sacrifice for sustainability, as will advances in the quality of individuals and communities.

While some goals related to the quality of relations are in critical ways threatened by the market, others, like creativity and individuality, are rewarded and encouraged.[40] And of course, improvements in productivity make it easier to afford expenditures to improve the quality of relations. A greater sense of equity can increase one's self-respect and one's awareness of the importance of appropriate communal ties. Enhancements in sustainability benefit the quality of relations in that they serve to prevent the social dislocations that would surely follow upon environmentally induced economic crises.

Conclusion

In summary, the economic life of a nation can be thought of as entailing four separable problems: allocation, distribution, scale, and the quality of relations. The primary attraction of markets has been their unprecedented success in the allocation of resources. Relying upon

Depedri, "Interpersonal Relations, Job Tenure and Job Satisfaction in Organizations: Some Empirical Results in Social and Community Care Services," available at http://www.aiel.it/bacheca/Firenze/Papers/Borzaga`Depedri.pdf.

[40] Few commentators have spoken so strongly about the positive effects of economic growth on the quality of persons and communities as has Michael Novak. See, for example, Michael Novak, *Spirit of Democratic Capitalism* (New York: The Free Press, 1993), 15–16.

and rewarding self-interested activity of individuals and organizations have led to the greatest outburst of economic productivity in the history of humankind. As Bernard Mandeville put it nearly three centuries ago, the system is one where "the very Poor Lived better than the Rich before."[41]

From a moral point of view, this favorable consequence is significant and weighs heavily in favor of a generally "free" market. Still, there are negative effects of the system, and these weigh heavily on the other side of the scale. Regardless of each citizen's assessment of the balance, it must be admitted that the productive process, here referred to as allocation, is but one of the basic problems to be addressed in setting the rules of the game for economic life. And although many forms of self-interested activity deserve an endorsement within the process of allocation, the extrapolation of the legitimacy of self-interested behavior outside the allocation process cannot rely on arguments that it helps allocative efficiency. This begs the question.

This framework of four problems is designed to organize, distinguish, and interrelate the basic problems facing any modern economy. It cannot of itself resolve the truly critical questions about what should be the relative weights of the four or even what should be the relative importance of the various values and goals implicit within each one. To take just one example, the philosophers Robert Nozick[42] and Michael Walzer[43] have widely divergent views on the relation of individual and community, and the framework of this chapter does not adjudicate their differences. The point of this schema is to sort out the four problems from one another and to provide a way to get all four sets of issues on the table when some parties to the economic policy debate conveniently forget about the other three problems in their enthusiasm for solutions to one of them.

Any attempt to simplify the complexities of life to improve our understanding entails the imposition of a structure. Thus, the schema of four problems of economic life to be presented here cannot hope to outline the issues in any universally valid manner. It represents a

[41] Bernard Mandeville, "The Grumbling Hive: or Knaves Turn'd Honest," in *The Fable of the Bees*, ed. Philip Harth (London: Penguin, 1970): 69.
[42] See Robert Nozick, *Anarchy, State and Utopia*, (Oxford: Blackwell, 1974).
[43] See Michael Walzer, *Spheres of Justice: A Defense of Pluralism and Equality* (New York: Basic Books, 1983).

perspective on the issues that will be helpful in advancing the dialogue between defenders and critics of the economic system prevailing in most of the Western world today. Readers on the right may object because it assigns facticity, or too much facticity, to social entities and underplays the roles and rights of individuals. Others further to the left may find it dangerous because it grants too much to the neo-conservative argument in favor of the effectiveness of market capitalism.

In addition, moral issues that include but also transcend economic activity are represented somewhat inaccurately when viewed solely from an economic perspective. For example, summarizing a multitude of moral issues under a general frame like "the quality of relations" clearly leaves racism, sexism, and many other particular issues unarticulated. This typology also exhibits the deficiencies inherent in focusing on the national economy, rather than international, and on the industrialized countries rather than the Third World, although the basic interdependencies among the four problems can be witnessed in those settings as well.

In spite of such shortcomings, addressing these four basic problems can lead to more careful study of the tradeoffs and interdependencies that exist among and between our most basic goals in economic life. No moral evaluation of markets can be complete otherwise.

PART II

THE MORAL ECOLOGY OF MARKETS

6

The Market as an Arena of Freedom

Are markets just?

As tempting as this question is, we should not ask it. The question is a mistake. Not a small mistake. And not simply a mistake from a scholar's point of view.

In spite of much good insight, the thousands of letters to the editors, op-ed pieces, scholarly articles, and books that have been written to answer the question "Are markets just?" have too often hurt our ability to evaluate markets from a moral perspective.

On the one hand, the question has generated simplicities on all sides that have undercut a real dialogue on the issue. Each oversimplification gives the "other side" more reason to give up any hope of a real conversation about the matter. And there is indeed a scandalous absence of authentic conversation about the morality of markets. Commentators on the left and right rarely engage each other's work and often don't even bother to read what their opponents have written, except to deride what they perceive to be the others' weakest arguments.

On the other hand, this question has effectively distracted both scholars and the general public from debates about the real issues that divide us.

The Importance of Context: Ecology

Any analysis of the morality of markets should begin with the recognition that no human institution – not even one as broad as the market – can be adequately understood without reference to its context. It is impossible to evaluate the justice of markets by looking at markets alone.

In this regard, we can helpfully borrow a concept from biology, where it is universally recognized that no single species of plant or animal can be understood without reference to its ecology, the pattern of relations between organisms and their environment. Biologists cite numerous examples, but among the more interesting is the sea otter in the North Pacific rim. These members of the weasel family are coveted for their thick, rich pelts, dark brown with up to a million hairs per square inch. Nineteenth-century trappers prized the sea otter and claimed to be doing a favor for fishermen and others dependent on the sea for livelihood, because the sea otter feasts on sea urchins, clams, snails, octopus, and abalone. By the early twentieth century, its numbers were down to near extinction.

The Pacific sea otter was eventually protected by the International Fur Seal Treaty, and populations returned to normal levels along part of the Alaskan coast, though in other parts it remained largely absent. Investigating the differences in the two habitats, biologists were able to detail the effects of sea otters on the ocean ecology and confirmed what some naturalists had been saying all along. With the decline of the otter, there were few natural enemies to sea urchins, which then flourished and overgrazed the kelp forests on the ocean floor. This in turn had drastic impact on a variety of sea creatures dependent on the kelp or on kelp-eating species. Researchers found that coastal areas without sea otters also lacked some types of game fish, as well as harbor seals and even bald eagles.[1] The sea otter is now understood as a "keystone" species nearly at the top of the food chain, essential to the healthy interaction and growth of the entire ecosystem.[2]

---

[1] Yvonne Baskin, *The Work of Nature: How the Diversity of Life Sustains Us* (Washington, D.C.: Island Press, 1997), 29.

[2] For a description of the ecology of the sea otter, see J. A. Estes, M. T. Tinker, T. M. Williams, and D. F. Doak, "Killer Whale Predation on Sea Otters Linking Oceanic and Nearshore Ecosystems," *Science* 282 (October 16, 1998): 473–6.

The point of this biological example here is that it would be futile to attempt to understand the kelp, sea urchins, otters, or any of the other species involved in this ecosystem without attending to their interactions with all the others. This same principle applies to our consideration of markets, because it is similarly futile to analyze markets as either moral or immoral, just or unjust, without attention to the social, political, and cultural context within which any particular market exists. Our task, then, is to understand not only markets but also their moral context – what we might call their "moral ecology."

There are four elements of the moral ecology of markets. This chapter focuses on the character of markets, and the next chapter addresses the other three. All these elements are present, at least implicitly, in every moral evaluation of markets, whether endorsement from the right or criticism from the left. It is not the purpose of this chapter – or of this book – to provide a definitive moral assessment of markets that the reader is encouraged to share. Rather, the goal is to provide a framework for understanding the diverse positions on markets as addressing the same fundamental issues – but with different moral and empirical presumptions. These presumptions, it turns out, almost always concern how each position evaluates the current status of the four problems of economic life (outlined in Chapter 5) and the alternative policies proposed to address them.

And here we must again note the error of Friedrich Hayek's belief, shared by many others, that "the demonstration of the difference between socialists and non-socialists ultimately rests on purely intellectual issues capable of a scientific resolution and not in different judgments of value."[3] On the contrary, only when a moral judgment is joined to an empirical assessment can the competing claims about alternative economic systems be adjudicated – or even understood.

In her book *The Faces of Injustice*, Judith Shklar insightfully investigates the "*sense* of injustice" we experience when treated unjustly. It is not simply the scholar's dispassionate logic that determines what constitutes injustice, she argues. Rather, the experience of injustice – the perception of it – also shapes society's understanding of justice itself.[4]

---

[3] Hayek, *Law, Legislation and Liberty*, Vol. 1, *Rules and Order* (Chicago: University of Chicago Press, 1973), 6.

[4] Judith N. Shklar, *The Faces of Injustice* (New Haven, Conn.: Yale University Press), 1990.

Shklar investigates the difference between misfortune and injustice, noting that perceptions, culture, and even technology affect whether we categorize a dreadful event as unfair or as simply unfortunate. An earthquake may be a natural event, but a contractor's violation of a building code or a government's unnecessarily slow provision of assistance may lead the victims and other citizens to see this disaster as not simply a misfortune but an injustice as well. As Shklar puts it, "the line of separation between injustice and misfortune is a political choice, not a simple rule that can be taken as a given."[5]

Shklar further develops the sense of injustice by attending to a pictorial representation of injustice in an early-fourteenth-century fresco created by Giotto in the Arena Chapel in Padua, Italy (Figure 6-1). The predominant figure in this work of art is a stern Italian ruler sitting with his body facing toward the viewer but head turned impassively to his right. Beneath his feet on a smaller scale is a depiction of two soldiers coolly observing theft, rape, and murder. Giotto's message is clear. Although the minor figures at the bottom represent the violent forms of injustice that rend the lives of individuals, the indifference of the ruler, cold and cruel in his inaction, is the main theme of injustice.[6]

As we shall see, a helpful way of understanding issues of justice in the economic sphere concerns those abusive activities that government (democratic today, aristocratic in Giotto's time) ought to prevent. Here the line between misfortune and injustice is quite influential, and differences on this issue directly produce differences in one's view of what limitations on markets are necessary if markets are to be trusted as just institutions. Once we recognize that we cannot distinguish injustice from misfortune without the use of a moral judgment, it becomes clear that the differences in economic systems entail not just empirical but normative differences as well.

Given the variety of approach and presumption exhibited in various conflicting perspectives on markets, it is tempting but wrong to conclude that the arguments of the various sides to the debate are simply incommensurable, so different from each other that there is no hope for establishing an authentic conversation about the matter. On the contrary, the differences between left and right over capitalism,

---

[5] Ibid., 5.
[6] For a fuller description, see ibid., 46.

FIGURE 6-1 *Injustice* by Giotto

socialism, and the role of markets do *not* reveal fundamentally incommensurable arguments on the two sides. Everyone involved engages a common set of issues; the opposing sides simply provide different answers. But to understand those different answers, even those coming from social scientists who claim not to trade in ethical arguments at all, we must recognize that a moral argument is entailed when addressing any of the four elements of this moral ecology. Too many of the current participants in the debate over markets leave such moral arguments largely implicit.

The Right Question to Ask

The question "Are markets just?" defies an answer. It's like asking "Are U.S. courts of law just?" Deciding whether the results of opposing lawyers' arguments for the plaintiff and defendant will eventuate in a just outcome depends on more than simply having the right rules for judges and juries to follow. The justice of a court system is threatened when any of a number of things in their broader context is badly constituted if, as frequently happens in some nations, one can easily bribe the police to "misplace" incriminating evidence or can threaten a juror's family to induce a favorable decision.

Similarly, the question "Are markets just?" ignores the political, social, and cultural context of markets. And those who *have* provided an answer to this impossible question inevitably *presumed* a particular context. Those endorsing markets tend to presume the context of the industrialized nations of the West, where the majority of the working class shares in the prosperity that markets help to create. Those critical of markets tend more frequently to presume the context of developing nations, where economic prosperity is more often reserved to a smaller group of elites, with the majority of the population living in poverty.

We must instead attend to the moral ecology of markets, the pattern of interaction between a market and its context. The right question to ask in any moral evaluation of markets is: "Under what conditions are the outcomes of markets just?"

As we shall see, asking about the character of markets themselves is an essential part of the analysis – it is the first element of this ecology – but is insufficient. There are three additional elements to be considered in the following chapter: the provision of essential goods and services, the morality of individuals and groups, and civil society. All four are inevitably involved in any effort to evaluate markets. The force of this insight becomes clearer from a consideration of a moral assessment of the exercise of self-interest in ordinary market transactions.

Self-Interest and Market Morality

As we saw in Chapters 2 and 3, both the critique of markets and their moral approbation have focused on the role of self-interest in economic life. A number of formal studies have investigated the literature about this topic.[7] As Albert Hirschman has argued, the moral rehabilitation of self-interest that occurred with the rise of commercial society in the seventeenth and eighteenth centuries praised self-interest on the grounds that it was superior to a number of destructive passions that had been so dominant in public life, including inherited animosities and the desire for glory.[8] Here it will be more helpful to begin simply with two examples of ordinary purchases that you might wish to make. In each of these cases the question will be: Given your moral convictions about the world, ought you to act out of self-interest in your purchase decision?

First, presume that you are in the grocery store and have decided to purchase two cans of green beans. You walk down the aisle and find that only six cans are left on the shelf, and two of these are dented. There is no evidence that the seal on the dented cans has been broken and thus they may serve your needs as well as the other cans, which are perfectly intact. Nonetheless, you worry that the food in these cans might be tainted and you don't want to subject your family to the potential danger of food poisoning, even though the risk appears minimal.

The question here is: Which cans would you choose to purchase?

Clearly, the self-interested thing to do is to purchase two undented cans. On the other hand, many people aspire to a life of concern for their neighbors, whether based on religious or philosophical grounds, and here it is clear that if you take the two dented cans, your neighbors to come along later in the day will have a better selection from which to choose. Thus the self-interested thing to do is to buy undented cans, while the neighborly thing to do is to buy the dented cans.

---

[7] See, for example, Jane J. Mansbridge, ed., *Beyond Self-Interest* (Chicago: University of Chicago Press, 1990); Howard Margolis, *Selfishness, Altruism, and Rationality: A Theory of Social Choice* (New York, Cambridge University Press, 1982); and Milton L. Myers, *The Soul of Modern Economic Man: Ideas of Self-Interest, Thomas Hobbes to Adam Smith* (Chicago: University of Chicago Press, 1983).

[8] Albert O. Hirschman, *The Passions and the Interests: Political Arguments for Capitalism Before Its Triumph* (Princeton, N.J.: Princeton University Press, 1977).

Now consider a second purchase that you may want to make, that of a small throw rug for the entryway to your home. You go to the store that has the best selection of rugs in town and you find one stack of rugs at a lower price than comparable rugs in the store. All the rugs from which you might choose are good-looking, but this one variety of rugs is offered at a price 30 percent lower than the others'.

We don't usually know the details about the production process of the various products we buy, but for the purpose of this example presume you happen to know that the rugs in this particular stack have all been made by children working in conditions of slavery in another country halfway around the globe. Many people mistakenly presume that slavery has been eliminated in the world, but there is ample evidence of its existence, for example, in the sex trade in various countries, where young women and girls are kidnapped from their home areas, taken across international borders and sold, sometimes several times in succession, from one brothel to another.[9] There are other examples of parents in severe poverty selling children into slavery and of the use of indentured servitude child labor in factories in some parts of the developing world. Thus, it is not outlandish to set up an example where we will presume you know that the children who made the rug you might buy are indeed living under conditions of slavery. The question at hand is: Which rug would you buy?

The self-interested thing to do would be to buy the cheaper rug made with the slave labor of children. Here, your neighbors will not be harmed if you choose to buy one of these rugs because a large supply is available and the vendor can purchase more at the same price on the international market. Still, perhaps you would prefer not to aid the unscrupulous factory owners who are abusing children even if all this happens half a world away.

If you are like most people, you will buy two undented cans of beans at the grocery. On the one hand, of course, this is a self-interested action, but that is not the primary justification to which one might appeal. Rather, if all shoppers at the grocery refuse to buy the two

---

[9] See, for example, Women's International Network News, "Tracking of Burmese Women and Girls into Brothels in Thailand," *Women's International Network News* 20 (Spring 1994): 34.

dented cans, we must ask ourselves what the grocery manager will do with those cans at the end of the week.

Most likely there will be a conversation with the employees, who may then receive better training about how to stock the shelves without dropping cans on the floor and denting them. Perhaps the cans were dented in the carton when they were shipped. In that case the manager may complain to the wholesaler and threaten to switch to a competing wholesaler across town unless the problem is eliminated. The wholesaler may then turn to the cannery that, perhaps, has a machine that has been denting every fifteenth can as it comes through. Here too the wholesaler may threaten the cannery with buying from a different cannery across the state and the manager of the cannery may then fix that machine. Here, with self-interest as the motive of the shopper, the grocer, the wholesaler, and the cannery, we can imagine with some plausibility that this problem of inefficiency, wherever it occurred along the chain of production and provision, will be addressed, reducing the resources allocated to food production without reducing the amount of food on people's tables.

This outcome need not depend on any commitment to higher principle but simply on all participants' looking out for their own interests. This, of course, is the logic of markets that Adam Smith celebrated more than two centuries ago when he observed that "it is not from the benevolence of the butcher, the brewer, or the baker that we expect our dinner, but from their regard to their own interest."[10] Self-interest need not result in harmful effects for others. It can, as is in this case, actually lead to a more careful husbandry of the goods of the Earth. Here we can improve allocation, the first problem of economic life, without worsening the problems of distribution, scale, or the quality of relations outlined in Chapter 5.

Now let us turn to our second example. Here, you may have concluded that in accord with your own values it would be wrong to buy the rug produced by enslaved children and instead opt to pay a higher price for a rug woven more responsibly. We rarely know the production histories of the goods we buy, but even many people who are willing

[10] Adam Smith, *The Wealth of Nations* (New York: Modern Library Edition, 1937), book 1, Chapter 2, 16.

to exert their self-interest in the purchase of the undented cans would step back from aiding and abetting an abusive factory owner.

If we consider only the problem of allocation, we would prefer that the lowest-cost factory produce our rugs. But here we must consider the damaging effects on the problem of distribution and the quality of relations. Employing economic analysis, we can observe that unlike the string of positive results from self-interest in the example of the dented cans, here we anticipate our self-interest to contribute to a series of effects whose overall result is morally offensive.

If we and many others purchase the cheaper rugs, this vendor will buy more of these and fewer of those others made in factories that treat their workers more responsibly. Those more responsible factories will eventually recognize that they are unable to sell their products because of the higher wage they are paying their workers, and they may be tempted to turn to abusive forms of child labor. And of course the factory that uses slave labor will then have an incentive to expand, as the demand for its products increases around the world. Here the chain of self-interested reactions to a consumer's self-interested purchase leads us on a kind of downward moral spiral.[11]

What is the difference between these two examples? Why is it that narrow self-interest in one seems to be morally praiseworthy, or at worst morally neutral, while in the other it tends to encourage some of the worst abuse of children in the economic system? The difference, of course, is in the institutional framework within which these two chains of events occur. In the first, there is a rough equality among shoppers at the grocery store and among retailers, wholesalers, and canners. Here, as Adam Smith pointed out, any seller needs to keep customers satisfied, and a dissatisfied customer often gets careful attention. We can improve allocation without worsening the other three problems of economic life. In the second example there is an immense difference in the status and power of the various participants in this chain of events. Those children in a far-off land are unable to break out of

---

[11] There are, of course, many important moral decisions to be made about child labor laws. They ought to differ in nations of considerably different economic situation. The point of the example here, however, is not to investigate appropriate child labor policy but simply to begin with a child labor situation that all readers can agree is morally offensive and then to ask what difference this makes for our confidence in markets.

an abusive servitude; letting self-interest reign would only harm them further. And of course, because in their efforts to address problems of distribution and the quality of relations nearly every nation of the world enforces laws against child slavery, in most of our purchases we don't have to think much about this problem.

We can learn two things from these examples.

The first is that there is no simple rule of thumb based on the intention of the actor that can determine whether narrowly self-interested action is good or bad. It is a mistake to believe that it is always wrong to act out of one's self-interest. It is just as serious a mistake to think it is always morally right to act out of one's self-interest in the economic realm. Neither view is adequate because the moral evaluation of any action in the market, whether or not that action is narrowly self-interested, will depend on the context and the results that eventuate. The economic defense of self-interest in markets is conditional, not absolute.

The second thing to learn from these examples is that markets are far from simple, uncontroversial, or spontaneous institutions that have arisen in human life. Although the interaction of individuals and firms *within* markets is spontaneous, markets themselves are structured by prohibitions against abusive activities that at least some market participants would undertake if not restricted by law from doing so. Of course, there will be debates over which activities *ought* to be prohibited, and these will be moral arguments. Everyone would prohibit child slavery; nearly all would prohibit indentured servitude for children; most would prohibit child labor in an industrialized nation; few would prohibit farm work by teenagers in a poor agricultural society. The point here is that whatever your view, you will judge markets to be morally reliable only if you agree with the prohibitions in place. This brings us to a consideration of how to think about markets if we are to evaluate them morally.

Markets as Arenas of Freedom Defined by Fences

What are markets?

Markets are highly complex institutions that vary widely in their history and operation depending on social, cultural, religious, political, and economic factors. Sociologists and cultural anthropologists distinguish between markets that are "embedded" in society (where social traditions and moral commitments severely limit the autonomous choices of individuals) and markets that are "disembedded" (where a diversity of perspectives and an interest in economic efficiency have greatly reduced the power of traditional restrictions on individuals).[12] In the modern world, governments have granted limited liability and the status of "legal person" to profit-making corporations and in the United States have even mandated that the fiduciary responsibility of corporate boards of directors be limited to serving stockholders' interests. These powerful economic organizations have grown dramatically and, enjoying the status of legal persons, have pressed those same governments to alter the rules of economic life in favor of corporate interests, causing both benefits for some human persons and burdens for others. Over the past century this complexity has increased significantly as the globalization of markets has rendered national control of the rules for markets more difficult to sustain.

In addressing the question "What are markets?", this book does not attempt an analysis of markets' historical and institutional complexity, as important as such an analysis would be. Rather, in order to make clearer several fundamental similarities of all markets, the book provides instead a relatively simple framework for thinking about markets that will assist the reader in sorting through the conflicting and seemingly incommensurable claims about markets made from left to right on the political spectrum. To do this it will be useful to introduce a spatial analogy.

With the development of electronic communications, many market transactions occur today between persons not physically proximate to one another. Still, it is helpful to think of markets with a spatial image from an earlier era, as a place where people come together voluntarily to make offers to others, always remaining free to accept or reject any offer they may receive. Employing this spatial analogy for markets, we can envision a market as depicted in Figure 6-2, an area bounded by a jagged fence that defines its perimeter. The sections of the fence represent laws, which restrict what is allowed to occur within

---

[12] For a seminal view of economic sociology and this relation between economy and society, see Karl Polanyi, *The Great Transformation* (New York: Farrar & Rinehart, Inc., 1944).

the market. "Abusive" acts are prohibited, excluded, and kept outside the fence by the threat of punishment. In some cases, economic exchange of particular goods or services is forbidden altogether (e.g., buying and selling body parts, children, the services of sexual partners or of thugs willing to murder your firm's competitors), and in these cases we often say there is no legal market at all for such activities. Or people sometimes say that society has refused to "allow a market" in body parts, children, and so on. The framework proposed here, recognizing that such a refusal is not always effective in preventing illegal buying and selling, speaks instead about laws attempting to "prevent such exchanges within the market." In some cases, the prohibitions of "abusive" activities take the form of regulations that forbid only certain ways of accomplishing a goal (e.g., practicing medicine without a license or charging too high an interest rate when lending money).

To harken back to the four problems of economic life in Chapter 5, we might note that there are many reasons why societies decide to forbid abusive actions in markets. A desire to improve allocation has led to laws against monopolies, fraud, and insider trading. Concerns for distribution have generated laws that prohibit offering very low wages (in sectors covered by minimum wage laws) and firing workers injured on the job (through workers' compensation laws). Efforts to address the problem of scale have led to laws against dumping city sewage into rivers or factory smokestack pollutants directly into the air. And work to improve the quality of relations in economic life has generated laws prohibiting the firing of women when they become pregnant, the discipline of workers by harsh punishments, and the sexual harassment of workers by superiors or peers.

Activity "A" in Figure 6-2, which might represent physical violence against one's competitor, is left outside the market by laws enforced by the power of the state. And similarly activity "B" may represent any prospective buyer's right to increase the price offered to a prospective seller, something that is perfectly legal. People enter the market and, with the exception of those activities prohibited by law, are legally free to use any means they wish, driven by any motives they may have.

Before going on, we should note the difference between "a market" and "the market." The former refers to any of a number of distinct markets – for corporate bonds, stocks, wheat, industrial equipment, or artworks. Reference in this book is almost always to "the" market,

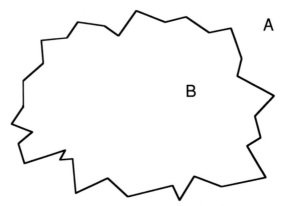

FIGURE 6-2 The Market: Defined by Fences

as that form of economic organization which allows individuals the freedom to do what they wish, to freely make and respond to offers, provided they avoid a list of abusive behaviors forbidden by law.

We now return to our question: "Under what conditions would we trust the outcomes of the market to be just?" Although conservative participants in the debate often endorse "free" markets, even libertarians agree that the outcomes of completely unrestricted interpersonal interaction will not be just if individuals are free to engage in force or fraud in market transactions. Such restrictions may help improve allocative efficiency, but it is important to note that libertarians would argue for them even if the prohibition hurt economic efficiency. Robert Nozick spends approximately the first half of his book *Anarchy, State and Utopia* trying to convince anarchists that national governments act justly when they restrict the behavior of their citizens in the prevention of fraud and the use of force.[13] Milton Friedman empowers government "to preserve law and order, to enforce private contracts, to foster competitive markets."[14] For Friedrich Hayek, the only thing "more important for everyone" than the benefits generated by the spontaneous order of society is "the security provided by the enforcement of the rules of just conduct."[15] For James Buchanan,

[13] Robert Nozick, *Anarchy, State and Utopia* (Oxford: Blackwell, 1982), Chapters 3–6.
[14] Milton Friedman, *Capitalism and Freedom* (Chicago: University of Chicago Press, 1962), 2.
[15] Hayek, *Law*, 133.

"once the limits of each person's rights are defined by agreement, economic interchange becomes almost the archetype of ordered anarchy. Individuals can deal with one another through wholly voluntary behavior without coercion or threat."[16]

When speaking precisely, even the most energetic proponents of "free" markets want the government to enforce some limits on what people are allowed to do.

Still, libertarians speak of "free" markets in a way that often leaves themselves and their listeners forgetful of this basic commitment to governmental prohibitions within their own argument. Here it is helpful to note in Buchanan's statement a circumlocution prevalent among libertarians that renders these very real fences around markets nearly invisible to them. Buchanan has just described the individual's market activity as "wholly voluntary," even though most speakers of the English language would say that if I am forbidden to arrange for the beating or murder of my competitors, my freedom is thereby limited, even if in a most appropriate way.

While not all libertarians employ this language, Buchanan and Nozick are not untypical in their argument that a person's action is "voluntary" as long as no other person has unjustly limited that person's available opportunities. For Nozick, no matter how severe the limitation that others' actions impose on my opportunities, all my subsequent actions will still be voluntary if "these others had the right to act as they did."[17] Nozick speaks of "voluntary" action and avoids the word "freedom," but Milton Friedman does not. According to Friedman, the essence of freedom is "the absence of coercion of a man by his fellow men."[18]

This is a peculiar definition of freedom. And the moral presumptions implicit in it unfortunately cloud the debate over markets. Applying Shklar's distinction, we might say that this interpretation of freedom conveniently expands the realm of misfortune and contracts the extent of injustice. This notion of freedom interprets the limits of nature – whether the universal inability of humans to fly or the

[16] James M. Buchanan, *The Limits of Liberty: Between Anarchy and Leviathan* (Chicago: University of Chicago Press, 1975), 18.

[17] Nozick, *Anarchy*, 262.

[18] Friedman, *Capitalism*, 15.

incapacity of most elderly people to run – not as limits on freedom at
all but rather as morally irrelevant constraints or, equivalently, as limits
on the alternatives available. Such constraints and limits are described
as not diminishing freedom.

The problems associated with this approach are well illustrated by
some peculiar situations to which it leads. If, for example, someone
is unable to walk because of a broken leg, we will need to know the
cause of the broken leg before we can decide if this person's freedom
has been limited. If the leg were broken in an accidental fall or during
a natural disaster, by the libertarian definition of freedom the person remains fully free (actions are "voluntary") even though unable
to walk. If instead a victim's leg were broken in a scuffle with a thief,
then the inability to walk due to the broken leg *would* violate freedom
(actions are not "voluntary") because the thief was violating the rights
of the victim in the attempted theft. However, if it were the thief who
broke his leg when an intended victim pushed him down the stairs
in self-defense, the broken leg would again cause no loss of freedom,
because the victim was within his rights in defending himself. And
because in many automobile accidents more than one driver is at fault,
at least to some degree, if a driver's leg were broken in a two-car accident, the libertarian definition of freedom might be completely unable
to tell us whether or not the broken leg would violate that driver's
freedom. This approach to the notion of freedom is at odds with ordinary usage, wherein a man with a broken leg, caused by whatever
sequence of events, has less freedom than he had prior to the injury.

One might wonder why so peculiar a view of freedom would be
employed. At least a portion of the answer comes from the role that
this definition of freedom plays in the defense of markets and the
definition of injustice. Because of the definition, Buchanan, Nozick,
and others can interpret the activity of individuals in markets as "wholly
voluntary" (or perhaps "completely free," in common parlance) in
spite of the obvious limitations imposed on market participants by the
prohibition against force and fraud. Thus the libertarian participant
in a market defined by libertarian fences might not even notice the
fences, because they represent no restriction of free or "voluntary"
behavior.

If, however, we are to come to an adequate understanding of markets and the debates about them, it is essential to recognize that in fact

there are fences around every market, even around the ideal libertarian market. These fences are indeed restrictions on one's voluntary choices that, if effectively policed, prevent abusive behaviors (again, as defined by libertarian standards) in the market. It does a great disservice to debates about markets when libertarian discourse about "free" markets renders invisible the fences even they themselves endorse.

All this implies, of course, that an essential part of the debate about economic structures concerns the lively debate about which activities are to be considered sufficiently abusive that they should be prohibited by law. Libertarians foreclose an essential conversation when they resolve this issue by a rhetorical technique. They define freedom to eliminate activities that libertarians consider abusive but refuse to prohibit other activities that their opponents consider abusive, on the grounds that these other prohibitions (but not their own) would represent a government restriction on freedom. Rhetoric from market proponents against government "intervention" distorts the conversation because when prohibiting abusive behaviors, governments are *constructing* markets, not "intervening" in them.[19]

In sum, even these far-right defenders of the market acknowledge that government-constructed fences are necessary to eliminate abusive behaviors. Contrary to popular perception, libertarians don't really believe in completely "free" markets. They understand that truly unrestricted interaction of individuals would be unjust.

Of course, participants in the debate with positions to the left of libertarians'[20] have a longer list of "abusive" activities that must be prevented before they can consider the outcomes of market interactions to be just. Some activities, like insider trading, are opposed

---

[19] Implicit here, but not developed, are the competing views of government itself represented by the diverse philosophical positions noted. For an insightful investigation of the difference between "private governance" and a more communitarian view of democracy by an advocate of the latter, see Douglas Sturm, "Economic Justice and the Commonwealth of Peoples," in *Religion and Economic Ethics*, Joseph F. Gower, ed. (Lanham, Md.: University Press of America, 1990), 17.

[20] Some libertarians are averse to employing the language of "the right" to refer to themselves, because in some of their positions (e.g., opposition to the legislation of social morality) they are closer to many parties on the left than to religious conservatives on the right. Nonetheless, because the language of left and right is so universal, and because it remains largely accurate in the areas of economic policy, with which this book deals, we will employ this traditional terminology.

on grounds of improving allocation, but most are judged abusive because of their damaging effects on distribution, scale, or the quality of relations.

John Rawls, for example, supports laws that would restrict the options of employers to discriminate against certain types of employees. He would limit the forms and amounts of bequests from the wealthy to their children and would restrict campaign financing in order to increase the worth of individual liberty.[21] The political scientist Susan Moller Okin proposes a dramatic alternative for reducing the typical power differential between a married worker in the market and a spouse who stays at home to care for the children: a requirement that the electronic deposit of the worker's paycheck be divided half and half into separate accounts for each spouse. Each would have "equal legal entitlement to all earnings coming into the household."[22] The abuse she aims to prevent is any mistreatment of the domestic caregiver, usually the wife, by the breadwinner, usually the husband, arising simply from control over the family's financial resources.

Further to the left on issues of economic organization, the communitarian philosopher Michael Walzer argues that factory managers exercise not just economic but also political power over their workers, in the sense that they control the "destination and risks" on the factory floor. As a result, he asserts, the selection of managers must be accomplished democratically, by vote of the workers, in any democratic society.[23] Claudio Katz, providing a "democratic" critique to "communitarianism," accepts "the modern claim that markets are both efficient and liberating," but like Walzer he would restrict the power of capitalist ownership.[24] And of course, Marxists have for generations argued that government needs to prohibit the private ownership of the means of production.

[21] Rawls, *A Theory of Justice* (Cambridge, Mass.: Harvard University Press, 1971), 83–9, 224–6, 277–8.
[22] Susan Moller Okin, *Justice, Gender, and the Family* (New York: Basic Books, 1989), 180–1.
[23] Michael Walzer, *Spheres of Justice* (New York: Basic Books, 1995), 291–2.
[24] Claudio J. Katz, "Private Property versus Markets: Democratic and Communitarian Critiques of Capitalism," *American Political Science Review* 91 (June 1997): 277.

Karl Marx argued that in capitalism the market actually makes a "fetish" of commodities. That is, economic goods, whose exchange should represent a social relationship among the many workers who produce them, instead take on a life of their own and become simply a means for profit for the factory owner by exploitation of the workers. But even here, Marx does not argue for doing away with markets altogether. He would restrict them so that the abuses of capitalist ownership cannot be maintained. Today the Marxian critique focuses on several shortcomings of markets that a democratic socialism would reduce or eliminate. These include that markets cause a perennial insecurity for workers, that they intensify economic inequalities, that they produce inevitable business cycles of expansion and contraction, and that they lead producers to respond to consumers' frivolous wants rather than to human needs.[25]

Each of these restrictions of economic behavior would entail the drawing inward of a fence to prevent some activity considered abusive.

This range of alternative definitions of what is "abusive" and thus of where we should construct the fences around markets is not simply the work of intellectuals but the real political process in every nation. For example, the Republican Party in the United States supports laws to prevent child labor, insider trading, and the practice of medicine without training and certification. Further to the left on the political spectrum, the Democratic Party supports the universal option for parental leaves upon the birth of a child, limitations on the prerogatives of firms to resist unionization, and further restrictions on property owners to protect the environment.

This understanding of a market as an arena bounded by fences that prohibit abusive behaviors represents a significant improvement over the simplicities about markets that tend to dominate both public discourse and economic textbooks. As we have seen, the standard texts for most introductory courses in economics often limit the options for economic organization to two: central planning and "free markets." But even central planners employ markets. More realistically, the

---

[25] Hans Breitenbach, Tom Burden, and David Coates, "Socialism, Planning, and the Market," in Thompson, et al., *Markets, Hierarchies & Networks* (London: Sage Publications, 1991), 49–50.

view of markets proposed here is relevant even within communism, as it existed in the Soviet Union. It is unproductive and misleading to describe the central planning of the old Moscow system as simply the opposite of markets. Rather, the Soviet political authorities considered far more activities to be abusive – for example, the private ownership of factories and banks – and thus they moved the fences much closer to the center. However, there was still a market within which freedom was allowed. After political authorities set up a system of restrictions and mandates, individuals acted in their own interests. Once Soviet citizens received their wages, they were free to spend their rubles as they wished.

Charles Lindblom, in his very helpful book *The Market System*, has argued that while markets exist in a myriad of eras and cultures, "a market system exists only when markets proliferate and link with each other in a particular way."[26] Yet in spite of his assertion that they do this "in a particular way," Lindblom himself runs up against the vast diversity of markets and in the end does not specify any line between market systems and nonmarket systems. The diversity of alternatives not only in theory but in practice around the world makes this distinction impossible to sustain. As a result, it seems more helpful to speak of markets as existing everywhere and having in different times and places differing sets of controls on them based on laws and traditions that provide their context.

Returning to the usual treatment of this issue in standard economic textbooks, we should observe that although there is an obviously important difference between central planning and markets, describing them simplistically as mutually exclusive does not serve well either students of economics or the general public. Central planners need markets, and markets are defined by government restrictions. The simple dichotomy so prevalent in economic textbooks focuses attention on the inferiority of communist economic systems. However, the economic debates that actually occur in the halls of government in the United States and in other industrialized nations rarely concern the

---

[26] Charles E. Lindblom, *The Market System: What It Is, How It Works, and What to Make of It* (New Haven, Conn.: Yale University Press, 2001), 4. Lindblom goes on to sketch out the details of a market system, with each such system requiring "liberty, property, the *quid de pro quo,* money, activity for sale, intermediaries, entrepreneurs, and collectives." See page 58.

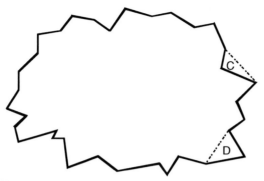

FIGURE 6-3 Changing Market Boundaries: Legalizing or Prohibiting Activities

relative merits of overall economic systems, such as capitalism or social-ism, but focus instead on the placement of fences. For example, some-one from the political right who argues that firms should have more freedom in dealing with their environmental wastes (represented as activity "C" in Figure 6-3) is, in effect, arguing that a portion of the fence should be moved outward to allow "C" in the market, making legitimate a previously illegal activity. Similarly, someone further to the political left may argue that firms should not be allowed to hire per-manent replacement workers during a strike ("D" in the figure). This means that a portion of the fence would be moved inward to prohibit "D," making illegal an activity currently permissible under U.S. law.

Conclusion

Markets are remarkable institutions. Most of their beneficial effects arise from the spontaneous interaction of individuals leading to results that no one could have predicted. The incentive to improve one's economic status is influential for inventors, entrepreneurs, and a host of others, including ordinary workers. And the spontaneity of interac-tions guarantees that when market conditions change (whether that's a large crop failure due to bad weather or the renewed availability of products from a nation that had previously been beset by war) prices will change, and this price signal will be quickly noted by market partici-pants far from the initial event. Still, we ought not confuse this spon-taneity within markets with the erroneous view that markets themselves are institutions that have developed spontaneously.

This latter view has been proposed by a number of advocates of "free" markets on the right, perhaps most famously by Friedrich Hayek, who has written extensively about the evolution of "spontaneous order." As we saw in Chapter 2, Hayek contends not only that activity within markets is spontaneous but that the development of the institution of the market was also spontaneous. He appeals to the example of the spontaneous development of common law under the hand of wise English judges over several centuries,[27] but the analogy would not seem to support his contention. Hayek's point, of course, is to argue that government should not tinker with markets, should not intervene in their orderly operation. There is, however, little doubt that the rules that define market operations today (the fences, to use the language of this chapter) have been debated and analyzed for centuries, with economists often taking an active part. To take simply one example, the repeal of the "corn laws" in nineteenth-century England (prohibitions against the importation of grain from the Continent) took decades of concerted effort. This move toward freer international trade could hardly be described as a spontaneous development.

Prior to judging the justice or injustice of existing markets, every citizen will have to decide where the fences should be constructed. However, the purpose of this chapter is neither to adjudicate disputes about where to erect the fences nor to propose a single set of fences that will "truly" render the outcome of markets just. The point here is that for any moral assessment of markets, it is far more productive to understand most arguments about economic policy as debates over where to construct the fences than as disputes about the merits of capitalism or socialism. People on the left tend to feel the need to restrict existing abuses while people on the right tend to agree with Buchanan that "little, if any, improvement in the lot of modern man is promised by the imposition of new rules by some men over other men."[28] Incorporating this pictorial view of markets circumscribed by fences into public conversation – and every introductory economics textbook – would go a long way toward shifting focus away from ideological simplicities and toward the real issues that divide us.

[27] Hayek, *Law*, 101.
[28] Buchanan, *Limits of Liberty*, 169.

In doing so, we might leave behind rhetorical devices that undermine honest dialogue. Those on the left should no longer speak of markets as simply tools of the powerful. Karl Marx identified the "world market" as the power that enslaves more and more workers.[29] All nations, even those centrally planned, need markets. The issue is the extent of freedom that will be allowed to individuals and firms within those markets. Similarly, those on the right should end their talk about "free" markets and their critique of "government intervention." Even libertarians agree that a literally free market, without any legal restrictions at all, would be intolerably unjust. Governments do not "intervene" in markets; governments structure markets by building the fences that define them.

Unlike the impression given by both left and right, there are not simply two kinds of policy proposals, those our sides endorses because they have only good effects, and those from the other side that will cause only harm. The rhetorical advantage deriving from simplicities such as these is highly prized from a "culture wars" perspective, but they undermine the prospects for authentic dialogue. The truth is that a vast array of policy options limit or increase the freedom of actors in the market and that citizens must choose among them based on how each affects the four problems of economic life. As always, this entails both empirical and moral judgments about existing problems and proposed solutions.

As we have now seen, if we are to assess justice in the markets, we must start with an accurate understanding of what a market is. Just as important, we must assess the context within which that market operates, and to this task we now turn.

---

[29] Karl Marx, *The German Ideology*, part one, ed. C. J. Arthur (New York: International Publishers, 1970), 55. We should recognize, of course, that not all Marxists speak so harshly about markets. See, for example, Arthur DiQuatiro, "Alienation and the Market," *American Political Science Review* 72 (September 1978): 871–87.

7

The Market's Moral Ecology

Every society's efforts to solve the four problems of economic life extend well beyond the definition of markets. As we saw in Chapter 5, even the preeminently economic problem of allocation is dependent for its success on a reasonable resolution of each of the other three problems of distribution, scale, and the quality of relations. Thus, although the proper construction of markets is the first element in the moral ecology of economic life, it is only one of four.

The Construction of Markets by Government

As we have seen, most economic policy debates about markets are best understood as disagreements about where to construct the fences that define markets, about which prohibitions or regulations ought to be employed to prevent abuses from occurring within those markets. This construction of fences is the first element in the moral ecology of markets, and as we saw in Chapter 6, this process of fence construction addresses all four of the problems of economic life identified in Chapter 5.

However, even if from any individual's point of view those fences are put in precisely the right places, there will not be a positive assessment of the morality of that marketplace without the proper context. Thus in addition to markets themselves, we must attend to three other elements in the moral ecology of markets: the provision of essential goods and services, the morality of individuals and groups, and civil society.

The Provision of Essential Goods and Services

The second element in the moral ecology of markets is the provision of essential goods and services, and this is quintessentially where the distributional shortcomings of the market are addressed.

This assertion might at first appear controversial because libertarians have traditionally denied that governments should engage in social provision. Instead they endorse "minimal" states. Responsible governments should simply enforce the basic rules against force and fraud. For example, Robert Nozick rejects the very idea of economic rights (e.g., a right to food, clothing, or shelter). "No one has a right to something whose realization requires certain uses of things and activities that other people have rights and entitlements over."[1] People have the right to complete control over the resources they have justly acquired, and so, for libertarians, taxation to fund the implementation of the economic "rights" of others is a violation of justice. Taxation is theft, or even worse.

Because taxation in effect claims for the state a portion of one's wages, it can be seen as equivalent to a claim on the labor itself. Thus Nozick asserts that "taxation of earnings from labor is on a par with forced labor."[2] As James Buchanan puts it, "I have repeatedly warned against thinking of the structure of individual rights in terms of an imputation of either final goods or units of productive capacity among persons. This is a pervasive error."[3] Both libertarians and their critics tend to see the libertarian perspective as denying that governments can justly tax their citizens to provide for essential goods or services needed by everyone.

This, however, is a misunderstanding. As Michael Walzer has put it, "Every political community is in principle a 'welfare state.'"[4] Even

---

[1] Robert Nozick, *Anarchy, State and Utopia* (Oxford: Blackwell, 1974), 238.

[2] Ibid., 169.

[3] James M. Buchanan, *The Limits of Liberty: Between Anarchy and Leviathan* (Chicago: University of Chicago Press, 1975), 86.

[4] Michael Walzer, *Spheres of Justice: A Defense of Pluralism and Equality* (New York: Basic Books, 1983), 68.

libertarians endorse the communal provision of those services they consider essential.[5]

Given the libertarian commitment to eliminating force and fraud, both a police force and a court system are essential for justice. If the police or courts are ineffective, force and fraud will prevail, and even libertarians would judge the spontaneous interaction of individuals in the market to be unjust. Thus, police and court services are paid for by taxation and are provided even to those citizens too poor to pay for them (and even if those particular citizens were too poor to pay any taxes at all).

Some libertarians, like Nozick, have used the terms "forced labor" or "slavery" to describe any tax on the citizens' incomes to pay for government services beyond the elimination of force and fraud.[6] Other libertarians, however, have a somewhat longer list of goods and services that should, or at least could, be justly provided by government and paid for by taxation. Milton Friedman has endorsed a negative income tax to help low-income persons, a taxation of the prosperous to transfer income to the poor.[7] Friedrich Hayek observed that, in addition to government financing of education for all citizens, "there is no reason why in a free society government should not assure to all protection against severe deprivation in the form of an assured minimum income."[8]

Others further to the left on the political spectrum have a longer list of "essential" goods or services that governments should provide.

John Rawls argues that two individuals with equal intelligence and equal willingness to exert themselves ought to have roughly equal life chances, something that won't usually occur if one is born to wealthy parents and the other into severe poverty. Rawls thus requires that

---

5 For example, Nozick, in his *Anarchy*, Chapters 2–6, constructs an argument against anarchists who would reserve the right not to participate in or pay taxes to Nozick's "minimal state." Nozick concludes that it is morally appropriate to collect (minimal) taxes from all who are able to pay to provide police and court services to all citizens.

6 Nozick, *Anarchy*, 169.

7 Milton Friedman, *Capitalism and Freedom* (Chicago: University of Chicago Press, 1962), 190–5.

8 Friedrich A. Hayek, *Law, Legislation and Liberty*, Vol. 2, *The Mirage of Social Justice* (Chicago: University of Chicago Press, 1976), 84, 87.

inner-city schools receive more tax dollars per student than wealthier suburban schools.[9]

From a communitarian perspective, Michael Walzer argues that every political community has provided, or at least has claimed to provide, "for the needs of its members as its members understood those needs."[10] Communal provision occurs because citizens recognize their common life and, as a result, the view that life as *lived in common* is deepened among the citizenry.[11] From this perspective Walzer argues in defense of guaranteeing basic medical care to all U.S. citizens, because such care is generally perceived as essential to contemporary life.

Once again, these differences among scholars are reflected in the debates in daily political discourse about what additional elements should or should not be on the list. In spite of disputes, such things as schools, city and national parks, roadways, emergency food assistance, and (with the exception of the United States) health care are items on which there is generally broad agreement in the advanced industrialized nations. Thus, consider the example of a woman who, through the misfortune of a traffic accident, is partially paralyzed and unable to work to support herself. Rather than leave her fate to the happenstance of neighborly charity, most people will judge that ultimately the government should guarantee that her basic needs such as health care and subsistence be met.

Beyond the list of what goods and services are essential, there lies the question of how and by whom they should be provided, even if they are subsidized by government revenues. This provision might be done through programs of local, state, or national governments; or the services themselves might be provided by private rather than state agencies. Few who believe people have the right to food think that the government should run the farms or grocery stores of the nation. Important moral arguments abound concerning the appropriate organization for providing such aid. Conservative critics of the welfare state have argued that it demeans the recipients of such assistance because its very assurance leads to a dependency upon it, reducing a sense of

---

[9] John Rawls, *A Theory of Justice* (Cambridge, Mass.: Harvard University Press, 1971), 73.
[10] Walzer, *Spheres of Justice*, 68.
[11] Ibid., 64–5.

initiative and self-respect. On the other hand, voices further to the left have argued that the uncertainties of voluntary charity, and the sense that those receiving the assistance can make no repayment to those granting it, actually threaten the recipients' self-respect. On this account, the needy are less humiliated in a system where they have a clear entitlement to assistance than when they are helped only at the personal discretion of those economically better off.[12] Here both sides are making arguments concerning the quality of relations.

In spite of differences over the method of provision, it is fair to say that for people on all sides, whatever the plan for provision, an obligation of the nation calls for assurance in law. Those in a large pluralistic society who really do intend to remove government support from all welfare services have, from the perspective of this analysis, decided that those services are not in fact "essential."

Let us recall *why* each participant in the debate includes the public provision of "essential" goods and services. Would Robert Nozick trust market interactions to be just if the innocent victim of fraud or theft could not turn to the police and the court system for redress? Would John Rawls have any confidence in the interplay of individual interest in the market if the least-well-off group in society were not guaranteed a "social minimum"? Would Marxists judge an economic system to be just if it did not provide jobs for all the able-bodied? Whatever goods and services that an individual might decide are essential, if those particular things were unavailable to persons who cannot afford to provide them for themselves, the economy as a whole would not be judged to eventuate in just outcomes. Without essential goods and services being available to all, the system would be seen as unjust.

Of course, there are radical differences in the rationales that different scholars employ in deciding which goods or services are essential. Nozick does not provide the assistance of the police and the courts to the indigent on the basis of a human right to such services. For him, in any development from a state of nature, the dominant private protective association, destined to become the national government, justly takes it upon itself to suspend every individual's natural right to self-defense and instead replaces that individual claim with the guarantee

[12] Avishai Margalit, *The Decent Society* (Cambridge, Mass.: Harvard University Press, 1995), 222–40.

that the government will provide the needed defense against force and fraud. The vast majority of individuals will see it in their interest to pay dues to their protective association voluntarily, and so this, from Nozick's perspective, will be a voluntary fee, not an abusive tax. However, because the services of police and courts are essential for the just treatment of each citizen, Nozick is willing to tax the reluctant (e.g., anarchists) in return for their benefiting from the service.

Unlike Nozick, others in the debate do often point to human rights as reasons for their own conviction that certain goods and services must be guaranteed. Not wanting to rely on *a priori* rights, John Rawls argues for a guaranteed "social minimum" based on his argument that neutral persons in the "original position" would define such communal provision as the most just policy to endorse.[13] Michael Walzer argues that governments are under the obligation to provide goods understood socially to be essential for their citizens.[14] And, of course, religious participants in the debate often point to a divinely based order as part of their rationale in deciding what goods and services are essential.

As the discussion makes clear, debates about this provision of essential goods and services relate most directly to the second of the four problems of economic life: distribution. But it has effects on the other three as well. For example, most economists judge that allocation is improved when business cycles are less severe, when economic "booms" don't go so high and "busts" don't go so low. Programs to provide goods and services (or the money to buy them) to the unemployed and poor entail rising government expenditures during recessions and falling expenditures during boom periods – a "counter-cyclical" pattern that dampens the extremes. Concerning the problem of scale, worldwide research has shown that as the income of persons and the average income of nations rise beyond subsistence, the willingness to pay for an improved natural environment also rises. And the quality of relations in economic life improves when the least-well-off groups experience a rise in material well-being, and the rise in self-respect and participation in society that usually accompanies this.

The main point of this section should be clear. Although there are disagreements about which goods and services are essential and why,

---

[13] Rawls, *Theory*, 274–84.
[14] Walzer, *Spheres*, 64–94.

all parties to the debate agree that the problem of distribution is an important one and that if the goods or services they consider essential are not provided (at the very least to those persons who are unable to secure them on their own), the outcomes of self-interested action in the marketplace will not be just.

The Morality of Individuals and Groups

The third element in the moral ecology of markets is the morality of individuals and groups, a major dimension of the quality of relations in economic life. Libertarians and others who defend individuals' rights to assert their own interests sometimes neglect the importance of individual morality beyond one's adhering to the prohibitions against force and fraud. The fact is that very few people would find markets morally attractive if all individuals sought only their own narrow interests and tempered this focus only in the face of laws limiting their activities.[15]

Interesting evidence for this reality appears even in the work of that most extreme of libertarians, Ayn Rand. Her novels celebrate rugged individualism and self-interest; her heroes explicitly argue that people have only the most minimal of libertarian obligations to others and that those who preach the importance of love and generosity are corrosive of the moral fabric of society. There are two obvious flaws in this wholesale rejection of the usual understanding of individual morality.

The first is that there is almost no reference in Rand's novels to that most basic of altruistic experiences in human life: the rearing of children. As Susan Moller Okin puts it, Rand and many other libertarians "take for granted that whole vast sphere of life in which persons (mostly women) take care of others, often at considerable cost to their advancement as individuals."[16] Okin chides Rand (and others who ignore the family) for presuming along with Thomas Hobbes that "just men spring like mushrooms from the earth."[17]

---

[15] Leland B. Yeager, "Ethics as Social Science," *Atlantic Economics Journal* 24 (1996): 18.
[16] Susan Moller Okin makes this point in her book *Justice, Gender, and the Family* (New York: Basic Books, 1989), 88.
[17] Ibid., 21.

Second, Rand's heroes, in spite of their ubiquitous claims to be concerned only for themselves, always happen to be highly principled, periodically empathetic, and at crucial times even kind individuals. Take, for example, Hank Reardon, one of the heroes in Rand's novel *Atlas Shrugged*. Reardon consistently claims to care only about himself and his business interests, but he often shows empathy for others and a willingness to contribute to their well-being – even when those others are so often portrayed by Rand as hypocritically preaching love of neighbor while actually looking out for themselves more astutely than Reardon himself does. That is, even the undeniable leader of the doctrine of self-interest on the right, Ayn Rand, seems to require as a part of being admirable that individuals display a high degree of ordinary morality in their daily lives. Although the minimal laws of the libertarian state would define the extent of any person's obligations, even for libertarians it seems that this is not enough for a humane economy. One does not need to be a Rawlsian to recognize that a person's sense of self-respect is grounded in the respect shown by others, both in personal life and in the institutional configuration of society.[18]

Economists purporting to provide a model for all of economic life (or in many cases, for all human decision making) too often ignore the role of morality simply because the model they choose to work with cannot easily accommodate such principled behavior. For example, although Buchanan refers to such virtuous behaviors as "analytically uninteresting," he is clearly appreciative of such "habit patterns" as respecting queues in supermarkets and extending "a sense of ordinary respect" for others.[19]

As Buchanan has put it,

Factually and historically, it may well be necessary that some notion of "social justice" or "social consciousness" characterize the thinking of at least some part of the population if a society embodying reasonable personal freedom is to exist.[20]

Although Buchanan's analysis sets out to resolve the problem of public choice without recourse to any societal moral consensus, he

[18] Rawls, *Theory*, 440–6.
[19] Buchanan, *Limited of Liberty*, 5.
[20] Ibid., 80.

does at points admit to the importance of broadly held moral convictions. "The social capital that a law-abiding society of free men represents can be 'eaten up.'"[21] We noted in Chapter 2 the libertarian inability to construct a moral obligation by citizens to improve political and economic institutions – and the inability of "value-free," self-interest models within economics even to explain empirically the fact that people often undertake such efforts. These "anomalies" can be explained only by admitting that behaviors beyond narrow self-interest are empirically important and that most people freely commit themselves to live up to duties even when these conflict with narrow self-interest.[22]

It is worth noting that even though many economists eschew moral arguments and rely solely on the individual's perception of self-interest as the motivating force in economic descriptions, others have provided an explicitly moral defense of markets that recognizes the place of the morality of individuals and groups. One significant example is the "Lay Letter" produced by a committee of Roman Catholic laypersons, headed by President Richard M. Nixon's Treasury Secretary William E. Simon and the theologian Michael Novak. Employing descriptions of nineteenth-century American culture provided by Alexis de Tocqueville, they argue that "democratic capitalism" relies heavily upon a spirit of cooperation and a concern for the common good that a narrowly self-interested attitude on the part of individuals or firms would thwart.[23] They argue for "the principle of self-interest rightly understood." They agree with de Tocqueville that virtue in the American perspective is useful and argue that it is in the interest of every person to be virtuous. A large part of this argument, of course, is that firms wishing to sell products must serve their customers better than their competitors do. "Democratic capitalism" is described as a general

---

[21] Ibid., 16.

[22] Recall also from Chapter 4 the moral inadequacy of the mainstream economist's definition of all human choice as self-interested, in the sense of serving to further the individual's goals, values, or interests. Not only in this usage does the meaning of morally responsible sacrifice of one's own interests evaporate, but it makes it impossible morally to distinguish Mother Teresa from the felon. The loss within economics is significant; the loss for everyday language is too great to allow.

[23] Lay Commission on Catholic Social Teaching and the U.S. Economy, *Toward the Future: Catholic Social Thought and the U.S. Economy, A Lay Letter* (New York: Lay Commission on Catholic Social Teaching and the U.S. Economy, 1984), 17–24.

system for the production of wealth that rewards those who serve their customers best.[24]

And as we saw in Chapter 2, even though Friedman, Buchanan, and Hayek tend not to make moral arguments in favor of markets, they ultimately employ moral commitment implicitly. They recognize that the moral character of individuals is empirically conducive to the effective operation of markets: Morality is essential for addressing the problem of allocation in economic life. There would be a tremendous loss of economic efficiency if the moral convictions of people evaporated. If honesty or hard work existed only because of threat of a penalty imposed by authorities, a far greater investment in monitoring and enforcement would have to be made – by each business and at all levels of government.[25]

Moving away from libertarians on the political spectrum, John Rawls distinguishes sharply between "the right" (the requirements of justice) and "the good" (one's view of what makes for a fulfilling human life). Rawls argues that a concern for justice should entail an examination of the former but does not require presumptions about the latter. His intention, of course, is to provide a view of justice that can be adopted by readers with a wide variety of philosophical differences in other matters. Still, Rawls argues for more than the minimum of legal requirements of morality. All individuals, after leaving the original position, are presumed to internalize the commitments made there and to live them out both in their personal lives and in the support they give to just institutions.

As we saw earlier, the reason for this is that human law is always a sort of "minimalist" expression of human morality. It sets a floor, or a moral minimum, below which human behavior is not allowed to descend. And there are a host of morally important activities that cannot be legally mandated without causing far more harm than good. Seven centuries ago, Thomas Aquinas cautioned that "human law cannot punish or forbid all evil deeds, since while aiming to do away with all

---

[24] Ibid., 23.
[25] For a recent example, consider the shifting attitudes in Germany toward the tolerance of bribery by German firms and other nations. See Peter Gumbel, "Germany Catches the European Disease: Corruption Is Spreading, as the Opel Case Shows," *Wall Street Journal* (July 13, 1995): A6.

evils it would do away with many good things and would hinder the advance of the common good."[26]

Consider the simple act of lying. While there are laws against lying in certain formal circumstances – such as in contracts or under oath in court testimony – there is no law against lying in daily life. The reason, of course, is that not only would the courts be clogged with legal suits pitting one person's word against another's but, just as important, the very fabric of everyday life would be threatened if people had to choose their words in ordinary conversation as carefully as is necessary under oath. If the maximum extent of human morality were defined by the law, we would be living in a barren world, one in which few would think positively of the economic system or of any other major social institution. However, most of us, most of the time, can count on our neighbors, co-workers, and friends to be generally truthful, to offer help when needed, and to show the ordinary signs of civility and cooperation – and at times real kindness. John Rawls argues that the minimal expectations of the natural duty of mutual respect form the foundation for the individual's own sense of self-respect.[27]

Libertarians are chary of positing any sort of personal moral *obligation* of citizens to improve justice in a society, often out of a concern that someone will then want to pass a law enforcing such conduct in violation of each individual's rights to choose how to spend personal time and resources. Nonetheless, libertarians surely prize a person's moral decision to work to further a libertarian view of justice. Rawls, on the other hand, argues that people actually have a "natural duty" to further just institutions, at least if such efforts are not very costly to the individual.[28] Judith Shklar observes how ordinary citizens are too often willing to buy peace at the price of injustice and argues that "there is no possible way to reduce injustice significantly without a massive and effective education in civic virtue for each and every citizen."[29]

Sociologists have historically identified various "control mechanisms" that operate within different institutions in society. In the market, price is the fundamental control mechanism, while within

[26] Thomas Aquinas, *Summa Theologiae* (New York: Blackfriars, 1964), I–II, q.91, a.4.
[27] Rawls, *Theory*, 337–8.
[28] Ibid., 115.
[29] Judith N. Shklar, *The Faces of Injustice* (New Haven, Conn.: Yale University Press, 1990), 45.

hierarchical organizations like corporations or governments, authority is the key. At the same time, however, sociologists also identify trust as a critically important factor, one actually recognized by some economists as well. Sociologically, trust may be defined as "the occasion when the probability that [another person] will perform an action that is beneficial or at least not detrimental to us is high enough for us to consider engaging in some form of cooperation with him."[30] Although many other economists overlook this important element of economic life, the Nobel laureate Kenneth Arrow summarizes the efficiency advantages of trust: "Trust is an important lubricant of a social system. It is extremely efficient: It saves people a lot of trouble to have a fair degree of reliance on other people's word."[31] Once again, if a basic level of trust among individuals within a firm or even between firms did not exist, a tremendously expensive outlay of resources would be necessary in order to monitor and enforce agreements. Morality affects allocation in addition to the quality of relations. And, of course, morality is also crucial in how the problems of distribution and scale are addressed. Different moral positions treat them in different ways, but all treatments of them entail moral commitments.

An analogous argument can be made about the morality of groups. Perhaps the best evidence of this is the effort that many business firms expend to shape their "corporate culture." As Lynn Sharp Paine puts it, "managers who fail to provide proper leadership and fail to institute systems that facilitate ethical conduct share responsibility with those who conceive, execute, and knowingly benefit from corporate misdeeds."[32] Mistrust and a narrow pursuit of self-interest by individuals or departments toward others within the firm are counterproductive, both for the profitability of the firm and for the employees' sense of meaningful work in daily interactions.

Stressing as we are here the importance of the morality of individuals and groups, it is nonetheless worth noting how decisions

---

[30] Diego Gambetta, 217, cited in Jeffrey L. Bradach and Robert G. Eccles, "Price, Authority and Trust: From Ideal Types to Plural Forms," in Thompson, et al., *Markets, Hierarchies & Networks* (London: Sage Publications, 1991), 282.

[31] Kenneth Arrow, 1974, 23, quoted in Bradach and Eccles, "Price, Authority," 282.

[32] Lynn Sharpe Paine, "Managing for Organizational Integrity," *Harvard Business Review* 72 (March–April, 1994): 106–17.

by individuals or individual firms are structured, conditioned, and constrained by decisions beyond the control of those decision makers. An individual may forgo the right to purchase pornography out of moral conviction, but we should note that in the United States pornography itself is available because of a First Amendment commitment to individual liberties. Out of a concern for just labor standards in developing countries, a college may decide to have its sportswear made in more responsible textiles factories, and it is able to do so because of the prior existence of an organization dedicated to facilitating this process. The president of a firm may decide on layoffs during a recession because of the fiduciary responsibilities to the stockholders of the corporation, but this stipulation that service to the stockholders must come first is not "natural" to corporations but rather is a product of U.S. corporate law. Many thriving corporations in Western European nations operate under a "co-determination" requirement, stipulating that up to half of the board of directors of each large corporation be elected by the workers. In such a situation, no preferential responsibility to stockholders over workers exists. Individual choice is important but is always influenced by its context.

There remain many questions as to what exactly ought to be the moral principles employed by individuals and groups within markets. The point here, as earlier, is not to identify those particular principles that are most appropriate but to argue that every moral evaluation of the market must engage, at least implicitly, this third element in the moral ecology. Each participant in the debate over markets will make a progressively more negative evaluation of the morality of any economy to the extent that important moral principles (however defined by that participant) are ignored in daily economic life.

The Presence of a Vibrant Civil Society

The final element in the moral ecology of markets is the presence of a vital network of voluntary associations that is often termed "civil society." Civil society includes a vast array of organizations larger than the family unit but smaller than the state, such as the fraternal clubs, houses of worship, parent/teacher associations, veterans' organizations, chambers of commerce, labor unions, hobbyists' associations, and a myriad of other groups.

Almost as diverse as the organizations of civil society themselves are the interpretations of civil society according to various viewpoints along the political spectrum. As Adam Seligman has put it, "right, left, and center, North, South, East, and West – civil society is identified with everything from multi-party systems and the rights of citizenship to individual volunteerism and the spirit of community."[33] Every perspective on markets, from adulation to condemnation, has been aligned with an endorsement of civil society, in at least one of its meanings.

Individuals join such voluntary associations to further their interests – at times more narrowly construed, at times in honest attempts to promote the common good. Many of these organizations are themselves involved in the decisions about where to locate the fences around markets or about the provision of essential goods and services, and nearly all are influential in the cultivation of civic virtue. Thus they are critically important for the appropriate resolution of the first three elements of the moral ecology of markets. And various civil society organizations have been set up to address each of the four problems of economic life: allocation, distribution, scale, and quality of relations.

Beyond that, however, the organizations of civil society are widely recognized as an essential training ground for an effective democratic process and thus also address the issue of reproduction of the quality of relations. As Mary Ann Glendon has put it, "a regime of self-government must have an adequate supply of citizens who are skilled in the arts of self-government – deliberation, compromise, consensus-building, civility, reason-giving."[34] People do not learn the skills of democracy by entering a voting booth. They learn them originally in their family of origin and then in a lifetime of participation in the institutions of civil society.

Libertarians address civil society less frequently than those who are further to the left on the political spectrum. Loren Lomasky

---

[33] Adam B. Seligman, "Civil Society as Idea and Ideal," in Simeon Chambers and Will Kylmlicka, eds., *Alternative Conceptions of Civil Society* (Princeton, N.J.: Princeton University Press, 2002), 13.

[34] Mary Ann Glendon, "Forgotten Questions: Introduction," in Mary Ann Glendon and David Blankenhorn, eds., *Seed Beds of Virtue: Sources of Competence, Character, and Citizenship in American Society* (Lanham, Md.: Madison Books, 1995), 3–4.

acknowledges the "lack of attention to the concept of civil society" and attributes that phenomenon to liberalism's broader conviction that neither government nor liberalism itself should attempt to tell people what to do.[35] Nonetheless, civil society is deemed essential by nearly all libertarians. Although libertarians are often accused of holding an atomistic conception of the human person, they clearly recognize the nearly ubiquitous tendency of humans to cooperate with one another to accomplish their goals.[36] Similarly, civil society is critical in resistance to totalitarian governments, as Hayek has argued; totalitarian states hold as a high priority the elimination of the organizations of civil society. "The true liberal must on the contrary desire as many as possible of those 'particular societies within the state,' voluntary organizations between the individual and government."[37] When individual citizens have no way to organize, there is little resistance to national totalitarian control.

Some libertarians have celebrated the breakdown of traditional community cohesion and lauded the de-personalization created in modern society. In his praise for the abstract standards of justice in the "open society," Hayek argues that "the rise of the ideal of impersonal justice based on formal rules has been achieved in a continuous struggle against those feelings of personal loyalty which provide the basis of the tribal society."[38] Similarly, Lomasky has argued that

such depersonalization is a good thing. It is protective of privacy.... Moreover, depersonalization undercuts invidious grounds of discrimination.... Whether that vendor is of the same religion or race or sexual preference as oneself becomes immaterial. This is not to maintain, of course, that a capitalistic economy is immune from the perversities of prejudice, but it is to note that these all-too-common feelings are meliorated by an impersonal price system.[39]

---

[35] Loren E. Lomasky, "Classical Liberalism and Civil Society," Chapter 3 in Simone Chambers and Will Kymlicka, eds., *Alternative Conceptions*, 51.

[36] In fact, Robert Nozick chides John Rawls for presuming that all the benefits of "social cooperation" are attributable to the governmentally organized cooperation in society. Nozick argues that a sizeable proportion of the benefits of modern society would be generated voluntarily even in the absence of government. Nozick does not mention civil society at this juncture, but that is certainly included in his intent. Nozick, *Anarchy*, 183–9.

[37] Hayek, *Law*, vol. 2, 150–1.

[38] Ibid., 143.

[39] Lomasky, *Classical Liberalism*, 63.

At the same time, however, libertarians are generally careful to note that it is the disappearance of the objectionable parts of traditional cultures that they celebrate. Beyond the prohibition of force and fraud, they are critical of the various conceptions of the good that individuals may pursue through government. As Lomasky has put it, liberal theory has not much attended to "love, beauty, athletic prowess, wonderful palate-caressing properties of a classic burgundy, poetry or, for that matter, metaphysics." Similarly, liberals' silence about the character of civil society "should not be interpreted as hostility."[40]

The endorsement of civil society from philosophical perspectives to the left of libertarians is both more robust and more detailed. Where libertarians understand civil society as a freely chosen association to accomplish one's goals, communitarian perspectives instead see civil society, at least in its ideal form, as "a realm of free choice, community, and participation."[41] That is, communitarians understand what happens in civil society as arising from and creating a stronger sense of cohesion and common identity than libertarians would recognize. As Michael Walzer puts it, "multiple and overlapping memberships help tie all to the group . . . together creating something larger and more encompassing than any of them. This larger entity is still a particular grouping – namely the civil society of a country."[42]

From this perspective, then, civil society plays an even more important role than it does for libertarians. Civil society becomes a reaction against the dissolution of the bonds of community weakened by both the impersonality of the market and the philosophy of impersonal human relations endorsed at least implicitly by libertarians. This is an old concern. As Jean Bethke Elshtain argues, both Alexis de Tocqueville in the nineteenth century and the anti-Federalists in the previous century resisted a tendency in modern life "in which highly self-interested individualists, disarticulated from the constraints and nurture of over-lapping associations of social life, require more and more checks, balances and controls from above in order that the

---

[40] Ibid., 64.
[41] Michael Walzer, "Equality and Civil Society," in Chambers and Kymlicka, *Alternative Conceptions*, Chapter 2, 37.
[42] Ibid., 36.

disintegrative effects of untrammeled individualism be at least somewhat muted in practice."[43]

Communitarian critiques of the breakdown of republican virtues
argue that much more than the organizations of civil society are necessary to reestablish the public philosophy necessary to secure even
constitutional liberties in the long run. Michael Sandal has argued that
the shift in both legal philosophy and public culture toward a more
individualistic view of self and government undermines the foundations on which a democratic republic stands.[44] The lineage of this
argument, of course, runs deep in history, back to classical Athenian
views of citizenship. Nonetheless, even for communitarians the experience of common goals and struggles gained within the institutions of
civil society can assist in developing the kind of republican consciousness they endorse.

Even further to the left is a version of civil society that Karl Marx
envisioned, at least in his more humanistic moments. Here creative
men and women are engaged in useful production not for the narrow
goal of economic survival but rather, in the ideal prosperous socialist
state, "for the sake of creativity itself, the highest expression of our
'species being' as *homo faber*, man the maker."[45] Under capitalism men
and women are forced to work in demeaning employment: under a
more humane economic structure, they would voluntarily engage one
another in production for both mutual need and self-expression.

Two other important contemporary perspectives on civil society
deserve mention here, both appreciative of its importance but more
skeptical about its potential than either the libertarian or communitarian. Feminists acknowledge the importance of civil society in
daily life but argue that "civil society remains gendered and exclusion-
ary."[46] Feminists tend to see the patterns of gender-based power in the
state and the family being replicated in civil society. In a similar way,

---

43 Jean Bethke Elshtain, "In Common Together: Unity, Diversity, and Civic Virtue," in
   Michael Walzer, ed., *Toward a Global Civil Society* (Providence, R.I.: Berghahn Books,
   1995), 81.
44 Michael J. Sandal, *Democracy's Discontent: America in Search of a Public Philosophy*
   (Cambridge, Mass.: Harvard University Press), 1996.
45 Michael Walzer, "The Concept of Civil Society," in Michael Walzer, ed., *Global Civil
   Society*, 11.
46 Anne Phillips, "Feminism and Civil Society," in Chambers and Kymlicka, *Alternative
   Conceptions*, Chapter 4, 76.

contemporary Marxists remind the proponents of civil society that it was Marx who early on argued that the guarantee of equal rights before the law only diverted attention away "from the site of real inequality: civil society."[47] It is in this panoply of organizations, including economic ones, that life is lived and where the oppression of ordinary citizens takes place. Nonetheless, we should note that both feminists and contemporary Marxists tend to hold out more hope for the attainment of greater equality in civil society than in government at any level.

The argument in this volume, then, is that civil society is an essential part of the moral ecology of economic markets and that no one will have confidence that the interactions of self-interest in markets will be just if markets operate without a well-functioning civil society. As we have seen, different perspectives define good functioning in different ways, but, just as with the other elements in the moral ecology of markets, any moral assessment of markets will depend on some moral assessment of civil society more broadly. In addition, without a vibrant civil society there is little hope that even a democratically structured government will in fact be responsive to the moral convictions of its citizens when resolving the questions implicit in the first three elements of the moral ecology of markets. As Peter Berger has put it, "mediating structures are essential for a vital democratic society."[48]

This interplay of civil society and economy helps explain the mixed reception that appeals for freer trade have received in the developing world. Because the moral assessment of markets depends also upon the other elements in this moral ecology, the absence of voluntary associations that make up a civil society is one of the primary cultural impediments to morally adequate economic systems in many developing nations. To take but one example, much of Latin Americans' skepticism about free trade can be seen as embodied in the responses of small-business owners of Buenos Aires, Argentina, who are largely unorganized and unrepresented in civil society, unlike their counterparts in the United States and Europe. They felt powerless and were largely ineffective against the neo-liberal economic policy decisions

---

[47] Simone Chambers, "A Critical Theory of Civil Society," in Chambers and Kymlicka, *Alternative Conceptions*, Chapter 5, 107.

[48] Peter L. Berger and Richard John Neuhaus, *To Empower People: The Role of Mediating Structures in Public Policy* (Washington, D.C.: American Enterprise Institute for Public Policy Research, 1977), 6.

of the regime of Carlos Menem in the 1990s. Not only were their economic prospects severely damaged by the abrupt arrival of multi-national retailers such as Wal-Mart, they were equally powerless in insisting on anti-corruption standards in national political life.[49]

This insight into the essential presence of a vibrant civil society before the outcomes of markets will be deemed just is but one of the important implications of this understanding of the moral ecology of markets. The justice of markets cannot be assessed except in their moral contexts.

Conclusion

We cannot assess markets, or even comprehend them, in isolation. As with the Pacific sea otter, we really understand the market only when we examine it within its political, social, and cultural context. When our purpose is to make a moral evaluation of this economic institution, we must attend to the moral ecology of markets.

Presume for a moment that two nations – your own and another – have identical prohibitions of abusive activities, by means of the same laws and regulations constructing the fences that form the market's perimeter. Presume also that those fences accord with your own view of where those fences should be placed, of exactly which activities are abuses that should be prevented within the market. The markets in these two nations are structured as you believe they should be.

But now presume that there are significant differences between the two nations in the other three elements of the market's moral ecology. From your point of view, your own nation has all three elements struc-tured exactly as you believe they should be, but the second is woefully inadequate.

If you are a libertarian, and if the second nation provides adequate police services to some citizens but does not protect the members of some particular racial group from theft and fraud, you will not have confidence that the free interaction of individuals in the market will be just. Without the provision of police services you consider essential to justice, it is quite likely that this racial group will be treated unjustly in

49 Conversation with small-business owners by the author, June 1997, Buenos Aires, Argentina.

market interactions. Similarly, if you're a communitarian and an individualist morality characterizes daily economic life in the workplace, you won't have confidence in the justice of the economy.

And no matter what your political orientation is, consider the situation where your society does not allow (or has no tradition of) a multitude of voluntary associations that make up a vibrant civil society. You will not have confidence that individual citizens can stand up to either economic or governmental powers when (your own view of) justice calls for a change of some sort in the economy.

In short, no evaluation of the justice of economic life can be adequate without attention to the complete moral ecology of markets. Or, to put this another way, every evaluation of markets that has ever been made has included an evaluation of the other three elements of the moral ecology of markets, at least implicitly. Usually implicitly. And this great silence about the moral context of markets is a prime explanation for the absence of a conversation between left and right about the moral adequacy of markets. Different people make different assumptions about how the market's moral ecology is structured, thus allowing them to come to different conclusions about the justice of markets – often with little awareness of the cause for those differences.

An awareness of the interplay of markets and their contexts is critical for understanding under what conditions the outcomes of voluntary interactions of individuals and businesses in the market will be considered just. As we have seen, the exertion of self-interest in economic life can receive a conditional moral approval; it will eventuate in just outcomes if markets have been properly defined by law, if essential goods and services are provided, if the morality of individuals and groups is apparent, and if there exists a vibrant civil society.

This is the "economic" defense of self-interest: a moral defense for the exertion of self within the properly structured context. Both free market advocates and Marxist critics can agree on this, even though they disagree fundamentally about where the fences should be constructed, what goods or services are essential, which morality is appropriate, and how to understand the institutions of civil society.

8

Implications

What conclusions, then, can we draw from this analysis?

This chapter summarizes what has been learned about the economic defense of self-interest and argues against its unwarranted use to justify lobbying. It briefly touches on options for individuals faced with living within an existing moral ecology of markets that they judge inadequate. It ends with a reaffirmation of the need for dialogue between widely divergent points of view.

Understanding the Economic Defense of Self-Interest and Markets

The defense of self-interest and markets entails a moral argument. We saw in Chapter 2 the unsuccessful attempts by the economists Milton Friedman, James Buchanan, and Friedrich Hayek to defend markets without recourse to moral argumentation. In the end, each required the inclusion of moral presumptions in order to complete his argument.

As we have also seen, that there is indeed a careful moral argument in defense of self-interested activity within markets – the "economic defense of self-interest."

As we saw in the discussion of social ethics in Chapter 3, two sorts of moral questions need to be distinguished. The first is "How should our institutions be structured?" The second is "Given the institutional structures within which I am living, what will I myself do in my own economic activities?"

Consider the first question. Deciding how to structure institutions requires conversations about the character of a market system, for example where to build the "fences" or what goods or services are essential. Such decisions are inevitably a mixture of empirical and moral judgments. Each person in the discussion must judge empirically what is currently happening and judge morally to what degree the current situation is objectionable. Similarly, each needs to judge what would happen empirically if a fence were moved inward or out, or if some particular goods or services were added to or deleted from the list of "essentials." Equally important, each will need to judge how significant the moral gain would be from such changes.

As we have also seen, it is essential to the economic defense of self-interest in markets that the legal restrictions represented by the fences around markets not be the sum total of moral influences on market activity. Without both the morality of individuals and groups and a vibrant civil society, very few will have confidence in the justice of self-interested activity in the market.

Now consider the second question, about one's personal economic choices within the existing institutional situation. Decisions about what any of us as individuals will do in economic life also begin in the context of these four elements. The penalties attached to laws are powerful incentives to obey, but individuals can – and some do – choose to violate the law. Moral norms and social expectations are powerful influences, but they are not determinative.

Rather, given the institutional context, people decide what in fact they will do as individuals and what values they will act on. For nearly everyone, this entails restrictions that lead them to avoid voluntarily some legal activities that would be in their narrow self-interest. Thus, individuals might chose not to purchase legal pornography, or colleges might chose to pay more to have their sweatshirts produced in factories with strong labor standards, or a firm might chose a smaller number of layoffs during a recession even though doing so will reduce profits.

This book has not attempted to propose guidelines in answering the second question about individual economic choices. It has focused on the first, concerning the structures. A conditional moral approbation for self-interest in markets is possible if the four elements of the moral ecology of markets are well structured. Of course, as we have seen again and again, different perspectives provide different answers to what is the proper structure of each of four elements, and this book has not attempted to endorse a single perspective on any of these four problems as the most adequate. The point has been to understand the character of the moral argument involved. Both critics and proponents of self-interest in markets are better served when they make explicit the various elements of their positions.

It is important to note that decisions on each of the four elements are heavily dependent upon the other three and no simple rule of thumb based on intentions or anything else can represent a formula for just markets regardless of time and place. In nations where civil society is vibrant and personal economic morality is strong, fewer abuses will need to be prohibited by law. Thus, for all the advantages of markets, it is morally naïve for proponents to argue that "free" markets (perhaps, those roughly approximating the fences of the U.S. economy) ought to be implemented everywhere without regard to the presence of the proper structuring of the other three elements in this moral ecology. To take but two examples, the power of organized crime in Russia after the fall of the Soviet Union and the long history of extreme government corruption ("kleptocracy," as it is often called) in a number of African nations present cultural problems that should alter the "ecological balance" among the four elements that every view of markets necessarily comprises, at least implicitly.

The key insight here is that the economic defense of self-interest – whether by Adam Smith or by contemporary positions across the political spectrum – does *not* simply claim that acting in one's own interest is just (or moral) regardless of context. It is just (or moral) only if the context is the right one, a judgment that requires both moral analysis and extensive social scientific investigation of the cultural and institutional situation. The economic defense of self-interest is conditional, and the conditions matter a great deal.

Lobbying Governments

As we have seen, the first and second elements in the moral ecology of markets entail government decisions about what fences to create in defining markets and what goods and services to provide even to those who cannot afford them. In a democracy, of course, these government decisions should reflect the empirical and moral assessments of the citizenry. Ultimately individuals do this by voting for one candidate rather than for another. Both individuals and organizations influence this process by expressing their views on particular issues and by spending their money, whether to help finance the campaigns of preferred candidates or to hire lobbyists to influence legislators.

What is often overlooked is that each individual and firm needs to examine the morality of its intervention in the political process. The role of self-interest and a concern for the common good in the democratic process have been long debated in political philosophy and democratic theory. The power of large corporations in modern democracies is immense, and as Charles Lindblom has put it, "they are too big and powerful to be servants and no more likely to behave as servants than would a giant in your household."[1] These issues and an adequate analysis of lobbying lie beyond the scope of this book.[2] But it is appropriate to address an all-too-common error related to lobbying: illegitimate extension of the economic defense of self-interest into the sphere of politics.

Many people often make the simplistic presumption that in the same way that an individual or firm may morally assert its profit-seeking self-interest in the market, it may also do so in the governmental process. This view, often taken by business leaders trying to influence government, represents a serious misunderstanding, because the two situations are quite different. The issue is a critical one, as U.S. businesses spend more than $1.3 billion per year on lobbying, six times more than all other sorts of organizations combined.[3]

As we have seen, the conditional approval for the exercise of self-interest in the market is based upon a prior judgment that the four elements of the moral ecology of markets are properly structured.

---

[1] Charles E. Lindblom, *The Market System: What It Is, How It Works, and What to Make of It* (New Haven, Conn.: Yale University Press, 2001), 67.

[2] For one review of the relation between self-interest in markets and in political life, see Henry M. Oliver Jr., "Attitudes Toward Market and Political Self-Interest," *Ethics* 65 (April 1955): 171–80.

[3] Federal Election Commission data released electronically on Wednesday, August 4, 2004, organized and presented by the Center for Responsive Politics, www.opensecrets.org.

However, when firms are involved in the process of creating the fences or deciding on public policy for essential goods and services, they are involved not within the market but in the definition of the market. Thus the conditional presumption that may exist within markets cannot be carried over to the firm's activity in the democratic process. The economic defense of self-interest is bounded. A simple example will illustrate this.

Suppose all the universities in the northern part of the United States decided to press the National Collegiate Athletic Association (the NCAA) to alter the rules for ice hockey. The proposal rule change would require that all hockey practices take place outdoors on natural ice. All official games could take place indoors, but teams would have to train outside. Obviously, if such a rule were implemented, universities in the north could regain the superiority they enjoyed before the invention of the artificial ice rink, which led to the rise of hockey "powerhouses" in regions where the climate does not allow for natural ice for more than a very brief period during the winter. We don't know, of course, whether these northern universities would have enough votes within the NCAA to bring about this rule change, but the question here is whether they would be morally justified in trying to do so.

The answer is clearly "No." But it is crucial to ask "Why?" Wouldn't this be simply one more legitimate way to "work hard" to field a winning team? Not at all.

The assertion of self-interest *within the game* allows each hockey team to play as hard as it can to win – so long as it stays within the rules, which, like our fences around the market, are designed to eliminate abuses. However, discussions *about the rules of the game* themselves are morally of a different nature from the exercise of self-interest within the game. The rules should treat all teams fairly and should be based on promotion of the common good. A proposal to require practice out of doors would unfairly penalize teams in warmer climates.

Even if, in accord with the economic defense of self-interest, individuals and firms have a conditional moral approval for the exercise of self-interest in the market because they do so within a well-constructed moral ecology of markets, they can never apply this economic argument to warrant lobbying or campaign contributions within the democratic process itself. The economic defense of self-interest has legitimacy only *within* the game; no economic grounds exist on which to conclude that any business is morally justified in pressing the government to alter the rules to favor its self-interest if that conflicts with the greater good.

There are, of course, important debates within political theory about the morality of lobbying. Some defend it as simply an expression of First Amendment rights, a sort of absolute freedom that ought not be constrained for any reason. Others condemn it for what they perceive as its detrimental effects on democracy. One study on the morality of lobbying has argued that the excessive expenditures in the U.S. political system "[undermine] political equality,"[4] the moral foundation of democracy. John Rawls has argued that the financial inequalities in the U.S. campaign finance system undermine what he calls the "meaning" of liberty. In one sense, this system leaves everyone equally free to contribute money. Yet in a more important sense, the weight of political influence depends not on each person's vote but on his or her income, a violation of democracy and of the guarantee of "equal liberty."[5]

These and other arguments concerning the morality of lobbying can and need to be made along with a political, sociological, and economic analysis of the forces existing in our current situation, something not addressed in this book. The point here is that it is a severe mistake to presume, as many do, that the economic defense of self-interest, whether from Adam Smith or anyone since, can help to warrant an argument in favor of lobbying. Because lobbying and campaign contributions have to do with the writing of rules of the game, the economic defense of self-interest cannot apply; its own existence depends upon the *prior* existence of just rules for economic life.

Economic Morality in an Imperfect World

Once we have a clear understanding of the four elements of the moral ecology of markets, it is quite likely that few people will judge that

[4] Woodstock Theological Center, Ethics and Public Policy Program, *The Ethics of Lobbying: Organized Interest, Political Power, and the Common Good* (Washington, D.C.: Georgetown University Press, 2002), 64.
[5] John Rawls, *A Theory of Justice* (Cambridge, Mass.: Harvard University Press, 1971), 221–8.

the moral ecology of markets within which they live is structured as they themselves would judge morally appropriate. At the same time, however, for the vast majority of people in the United States, there may also be a general agreement that most of the fences around the current market are morally appropriate to prevent abuses. Similarly, opinion polls show popular attitudes that although there is uncertainty about the extent of provision, a social safety net is a public necessity, that the morality of individuals and groups is a crucial part of human life and that the variety of voluntary associations existing in U.S. society is a great advantage, both individually and for the public good. That is, although few may judge the current moral ecology of markets in the United States to be perfect, very few would judge it to be so unjust as to require nonparticipation.

So what do you do if you judge that the current system is not properly structured and yet does not call for an outright rebellion either?

Clearly one of the approaches is to be thoughtful in the application of the moral approbation of self-interest that this defense of markets can provide. As we saw in the earlier example of the two dented cans of beans, in many situations a rough presumption of a beneficial outcome can lead individuals to feel free to act in their interest in the market. At the same time, there are other areas – often related to environmental damage, domestic poverty, and the well-being of the people of developing nations – where morally responsible market participants might choose not to exercise their legal right to act in their narrow self-interest but might instead choose, say, to pay a higher price for goods or services that are produced in a manner morally more appropriate than are lower-priced goods or services.

Perhaps the key element here is the awareness that the economic defense of self-interest is conditional and that when the conditions are not fulfilled, those persons who benefit from a system while others are either harmed or excluded bear some degree of complicity in whatever injustice occurs. This is not the vivid culpability of an individual who has personally decided to take an unjust action that harms another. Nonetheless, it is a sense of a shared responsibility for a system from which we benefit.

None of us can change the system through our own action alone, and too few of us feel we can to make a difference even working with others. And yet one key element of a moral response to the situation of complicity is an engagement in efforts to improve the system where that improvement is needed. At a minimum, in a democracy one can be committed to voting not simply out of self-interest but to elect persons who will work to structure better the moral ecology of markets within which we live.

Moving Beyond: The Need for Dialogue

The cacophony of voices concerning the morality of markets that we reviewed in Chapter 1 reminds us that there are few easy answers to the many questions involved. At the same time, however, one of the most discouraging parts of this "debate" about economic structures is the lack of real dialogue between proponents with differing views on the issue.

As Albert Hirschman has argued,

The systematic lack of communication between groups of citizens, such as liberals and conservatives, progressives and reactionaries, . . . seems more worrisome to me than the isolation of anomic individuals in "mass society" of which sociologists have made so much.[6]

The market is designed as an arena where people are left to decide individually what they will do in making offers to others and responding to offers made in turn to them. However, the discussion about the character of markets suffers only when conducted on the same individualistic model. It is a scandal that so many people, well educated or not, engage only points of view similar to their own. In the professional societies of many academic disciplines, those on the left and the right long ago stopped seeking each other out for criticism and now rarely read the writings of the "other side" except to find fault. All too many media outlets have become identified with particular political points of view. Newspaper pundits, radio talk show hosts, and a myriad of Internet sites "preach to the choir," not appealing for greater understanding of the issues at stake but rather forcefully making one-sided arguments that only those already committed to the conclusion will find persuasive. All too often each group describes the "other side" in terms those opponents would not recognize. Opponents are often misunderstood

[6] Albert O. Hirschman, *The Rhetoric of Reaction: Perversity, Futility, Jeopardy* (Cambridge, Mass.: Harvard University Press, 1991), ix–x.

as using arguments so different from the well-warranted arguments of "our side" that any kind of dialogue is presumed ahead of time to be fruitless.

In sum, the most fundamental conviction behind the argument in this book is that all participants in the debate about the justice of markets are already addressing the same four problems of economic life and taking positions on the same four elements of the moral ecology of markets. In spite of significant differences of perspectives, because we have common problems to face and a common framework in play, what we need is a common conversation.

Bibliography

Alford, Helen J., O. P., and Michael J. Naughton. *Managing as if Faith Mattered: Christian Social Principles in the Modern Organization.* Notre Dame, Ind.: University of Notre Dame Press, 2001.

Altmeyer, Arthur J. *The Formative Years of Social Security.* Madison: University of Wisconsin Press, 1968.

Altvater, Elmar. "Economic Policy and the Role of the State – The Invisible, the Visible and the Third Hand." In *Toward a Global Civil Society,* ed. Michael Walzer. Oxford and Providence: Berghahn Books, 1995.

Aquinas, Thomas. *Summa Theologica.* Translated by Fathers of the English Dominican Province. New York: Benzinger Brothers, 1947.

Ayer, Elenor H. *The Anasazi.* New York: Walker and Company, 1993.

Balbus, John. "Water Quality and Water Resources." In *Life Support: The Environment and Human Health,* ed. Michael McCally. Cambridge, Mass.: MIT Press, 2002.

Barr, Nicholas. "Economic Theory and the Welfare State: A Survey and Interpretation. *Journal of Economic Literature* 30 (June 1992): 741–803.

Baskin, Yvonne. *The Work of Nature.* Washington, D.C.: Island Press, 1997.

Bellamy, Edward. *Looking Backward.* New York: New American Library, 1960.

Bennett, William. *Our Children and Our Country: Improving America's Schools and Affirming the Common Culture.* New York: Simon & Schuster, 1968.

Berger, Peter, and Thomas Luckmann. *The Social Construction of Reality: A Treatise in the Society of Knowledge.* New York: Anchor Books, 1966.

Berger, Peter, and Richard John Neuhaus. *To Empower People: The Role of Mediating Structures in Public Policy.* Washington, D.C.: American Enterprise Institute for Public Policy, 1977.

Blackman, William C., Jr. *Basic Hazardous Waste Management.* Boca Raton, Fla.: Lewis Publishers, 1993.

Blank, Rebecca M. "Can Equity and Efficiency Complement Each Other?" Conference paper available at http://www.fordschool.umich.edu/research/papers/PDFfiles/02-001.pdf.

Blank, Rebecca M., and William McGurn. *Is the Market Moral? A Dialogue on Religion, Economics and Justice.* Washington, D.C.: Brookings Institution Press, 2004.

Borzaga, Carlo, and Sara Depedri. "Interpersonal Relations, Job Tenure and Job Satisfaction in Organizations: Some Empirical Results in Social and Community Care Services." Available at http://www.aiel.it/bacheca/Firenze/Papers/Borzaga_Depedri.pdf.

Bradach, Jeffrey L., and Robert G. Eccles. "Price, Authority, and Trust: From Types to Plural Forms." In *Markets, Hierarchies, and Networks: The Coordination of Social Life*, ed. Grahame Thompson, Jennifer Frances, Rosalind Levacic, and Jeremy Mitchell. London and Newbury Park, Calif.: Sage Publications, 1991.

Breitenbach, Hans, Tom Burden, and David Coates. "Socialism, Planning, and the Market." In *Markets, Hierarchies, and Networks: The Coordination of Social Life*, ed. Grahame Thompson, Jennifer Frances, Rosalind Levacic, and Jeremy Mitchell. London and Newbury Park, Calif.: Sage Publications, 1991.

Brennan, Geoffrey, and James M. Buchanan. "The Normative Purpose of Economic 'Science': Rediscovery of an Eighteenth-Century Method." In *The Theory of Public Choice II*, ed. James M. Buchanan and Robert D. Tollison. Ann Arbor: University of Michigan Press, 1984.

Broome, John. *Ethics and Economics.* Cambridge: Cambridge University Press, 1999.

Buchanan, James M. *The Limits of Liberty: Between Anarchy and Leviathan.* Chicago: University of Chicago Press, 1975.

———. "Natural and Artifactual Man." In James M. Buchanan, *What Should Economists Do?* Indianapolis, Ind.: Liberty Press, 1979.

———. *Ethics and Economic Progress.* Norman: University of Oklahoma Press, 1994.

Buchanan, James M., and Warren Samuels. "On Some Fundamental Issues in Political Economy: An Exchange of Correspondence." *Journal of Economic Issues* 9 (March 1975): 15–38.

Buchanan, James, M., and Robert D. Tollison. *The Theory of Public Choice II.* Ann Arbor: University of Michigan Press, 1984.

Buchanan, James M., and Gordon Tullock. *The Calculus of Consent: Logical Foundations of Constitutional Democracy.* Ann Arbor: University of Michigan Press, 1962.

Caldwell, Bruce. "Hayek and Socialism." *Journal of Economic Literature* 35 (December 1997): 1856–90.

Chambers, Simone, and Will Kymlicka, eds. *Alternative Conceptions of Civil Society.* Princeton, N.J.: Princeton University Press, 2002.

Clark, John Bates. *The New Philosophy of Wealth: Economic Principles Newly Formulated* (1877). New York: A. M. Kelley, 1967.

Cohen, Jean L., and Andrew Arato. *Civil Society and Political Theory.* Cambridge, Mass., and London: MIT Press, 1995.

Coleman, James S. "Social Capital in the Creation of Human Capital. *American Journal of Sociology, Supplement* 94 (1988): S95–S120.

Cropsey, Joseph. *Polity and Economy: With Further Thoughts on the Principles of Adam Smith.* South Bend, Ind.: Saint Augustine's Press, 2001.

Curran, Charles E. *The Catholic Moral Tradition Today: A Synthesis.* Washington, D.C.: Georgetown University Press, 1999.

Daly, Herman E. "Beyond Growth: Avoiding Uneconomic Growth." In *The Sustainability of Long-term Growth: Socio-economic and Ecological Perspectives*, ed. Mohan Munasinghe, Osvaldo Sunkel, and Carlos de Miguel. Cheltenham: Edward Elgar, 2002.

Danziger, Sheldon, Robert Haveman, and Robert Plotnick. "How Income Transfer Programs Affect Work, Saving and the Income Distribution: A Critical Review."*Journal of Economic Literature* 19 (September 1981): 975–1028.

Davis, Joseph A. "Ozone Depletion: When Less Is Not Enough." *Reporting on Climate Change: Understanding the Science.* Washington, D.C.: Environmental Health Center, National Safety Council, June 2000.

DiQuatiro, Arthur. "Alienation and the Markets."*American Political Science Review* 72 (September 1978): 871–87.

Donahue-White, Patricia, Stephen J. Grabill, Christopher Westley, and Gloria Zúñiga. *Human Nature and the Discipline of Economics.* Lanham, Md.: Lexington Books, 2002.

Eden, Phillip, John Weeks, and Lukin Robinson. "The Triumph of Capitalism? Three Responses." *Monthly Review* 41 (November 1989): 51–8.

Ekelund, Robert B., Jr., and Robert D. Tollison. *Economics: Private Markets and Public Choice,* sixth edition. New York: Addison-Wesley, 2000.

Elshtain, Jean Bethke. "In Common Together: Unity, Diversity, and Civic Virtue." In *Towards a Global Civil Society*, ed. Michael Walzer. Providence, R.I.: Berghahn Books, 1955.

Epstein, Paul R. "Is Global Warming Harmful to Health?" *Scientific American* 283 (August 2000): 50–7.

Estes, J. A., M. T. Tinker, T. M. Williams, and D. F. Doak."Killer Whale Predation on Sea Otters Linking Oceanic and Near Shore Ecosystems."*Science* 282 (October 1998): 473–6.

Fenton, Natalie. "Critical Perspectives on Trust and Civil Society." In *Trust and Civil Society*, ed. Fran Tonkiss and Andrew Passey. New York: St. Martin's Press, 2000.

Ferguson, William M. *The Anasazi of Mesa Verde and the Four Corners.* Boulder: University Press of Colorado, 1996.

Frankena, William K. *Ethics,* second edition. Englewood Cliffs, N.J.: Prentice-Hall, 1973.

Freese, Barbara. *Coal: A Human History.* Cambridge, Mass.: Perseus Books, 2003.

Friedman, Milton. *Essays in Positive Economics.* Chicago: University of Chicago Press, 1953.

———. *Capitalism and Freedom.* Chicago: University of Chicago Press, 1962.

Fukuyama, Francis. "The End of History?" *The National Interest* 15 (Summer 1989): 3–18.

Furth, Harold P. "Fusion." *Scientific American* 273 (September 1995): 174–7.

Garcia, Ismael. *Justice in Latin American Theology of Liberation.* Atlanta: John Knox Press, 1987.

Geller, Ernest. *Conditions of Liberty: Civil Society and Its Rivals.* New York: The Penguin Press, 1994.

Gever, John, Robert Kaufmann, David Skole, and Charles Vorosmarty. *Beyond Oil: The Threat to Food and Fuel in the Coming Decades.* Cambridge, Mass.: Ballinger Publishing Company, 1986.

Glendon, Mary Ann, and David Blankenhorn, eds. *Seedbeds of Virtue: Sources of Competence, Character, and Citizenship.* Lanham, Md.: Madison Books, 1995.

Gokehale, Jagadeesh, and Lawrence J. Kotlikoff. "The Impact of Social Security and Other Factors on the Distribution of Wealth." In *The Distributional Aspects of Social Security and Social Security Reform,* ed. Martin Feldstein and Jeffrey B. Liebman. Chicago: University of Chicago Press, 2002.

Gosling, Morris L., and William J. Southerland, eds. *Behavior and Conservation.* Cambridge: Cambridge University Press, 2000.

Gronbacher, Gregory M. A.,"The Human Economy: Neither Right nor Left; A Response to Daniel Rush Finn." In *Journal of Markets and Morality* 2 (Fall 1999): 247–70.

Gumbel, Peter. "Germany Catches the European Disease: Corruption Is Spreading, as the Opel Case Shows." *Wall Street Journal,* 13 July 1995.

Gwartney, James, and Robert Lawson. *Economic Freedom and Good Government.* Vancouver: Frasier, 2004.

Hansen, James. "Defusing the Global Warming Time Bomb." *Scientific American* 290 (March 2004): 68–77.

Harris, H., ed. *Scientific Models and Men.* London: Oxford University Press, 1978.

Haslett, D. W. *Capitalism with Morality.* New York: Oxford University Press, 1994.

Hausman, Daniel M. *The Philosophy of Economics: An Anthology,* second edition. New York: Cambridge University Press, 1994.

Hayek, Friedrich A. "The Use of Knowledge in Society."*American Economic Review* 35 (September 1945): 519–30.

———. *Individualism and Economic Order.* Chicago: University of Chicago Press, 1948.

———. *Road to Serfdom.* Chicago: University of Chicago Press, 1944.

———. *Law, Legislation and Liberty.* Vol. 1, *Rules and Order.* Chicago: University of Chicago Press, 1973.

———. *Law, Legislation and Liberty.* Vol. 2, *The Mirage of Social Justice.* Chicago: University of Chicago Press, 1976.

———. *Law, Legislation and Liberty.* Vol. 3, *The Political Order of a Free People.* Chicago: University of Chicago Press, 1979.

Heilbroner, Robert."Reflections: The Triumph of Capitalism." *The New Yorker* 64 (January 1989): 98–109.

―――. *An Inquiry into the Human Prospect.* New York: Norton, 1974.

Himmelfarb, Gertrude. "The Idea of Compassion: The British vs. the French Enlightenment." *The Public Interest* (Fall 2001): 1–9.

Hirschman, Albert O. *The Rhetoric of Reaction: Perversity, Futility, Jeopardy.* Cambridge, Mass.: Harvard University Press, 1992.

―――. *Rival Views of Market Society and Other Recent Essays.* Cambridge, Mass.: Harvard University Press, 1992.

―――. *The Passions and the Interests: Political Arguments for Capitalism before Its Triumph.* Princeton, N.J.: Princeton University Press, 1977.

Hobbes, Thomas. *Leviathan: or the Matter, Form and Power of a Commonwealth Ecclesiastical and Civil* (1651). London: Penguin Publishers, 1988.

Isbister, John. *Capitalism and Justice: Envisioning Social and Economic Fairness.* Bloomfield, Conn.: Kumarian Press, 2001.

Hollenbach, David. "Christian Social Ethics after the Cold War." In *John Paul II and Moral Theology.* Readings in Moral Theology, no. 10, ed. Charles E. Curran and Richard A. McCormick. New York: Paulist Press, 1998, 352–75. Reprinted from *Theological Studies* 53 (March 1992): 75–95.

Karl, Thomas R., Neville Nicholls, and Jonathan Gregory. "The Coming Climate." *Scientific American* 276 (May 1997): 79–83.

Katz, Claudio J. "Private Property versus Markets: Democratic and Communitarian Critiques of Capitalism." *American Political Science Review* 91 (June 1997): 277–88.

Keynes, John M. *The General Theory of Employment, Interest and Money.* London: Macmillan, 1936.

Knight, Frank. *Freedom and Reform.* New York: Harper & Brothers, 1947.

―――. *The Economic Organization* (1933). New York: Augustus M. Kelley, 1951.

Kukathas, Chandran. *Hayek and Modern Liberalism.* New York: Oxford University Press, 1990.

Lake, James, Ralph G. Bennett, and John F. Kotek. "Next Generation of Nuclear Power." *Scientific American* 286 (January 2002): 72–9.

Lavoie, Don. *Rivalry & Central Planning: The Socialist Calculation Debate Reconsidered.* Cambridge: Cambridge University Press, 1985.

Lay Commission on Catholic Social Teaching and the U.S. Economy. *Toward the Future: Catholic Social Thought and the U.S. Economy, A Lay Letter.* New York: Lay Commission on Catholic Social Teaching and the U.S. Economy, 1984.

Leibenstein, Harvey. "Allocative Efficiency Versus 'X-Efficiency.'" *American Economic Review* 56 (June 1966): 392–415.

Leslie, Thomas, and Edward Cliffe. *Essays in Political Economy.* London: Longmans, Green & Co., 1888.

Levitus, Sydney, John I. Antonov, Timothy P. Boyer, and Cathy Stephens. "Warming of the World Ocean." *Science* 287 (March 2000): 225–9.

Lewis, Thomas J. "Acquisition and Anxiety: Aristotle's Case Against the Market." *Canadian Journal of Economics* 11 (February 1978): 69–90.

Lindblom, Charles E. *The Market System: What It Is, How It Works, and What to Make of It.* New Haven, Conn.: Yale University Press, 2001.

Lindert, Peter. *Growing Public: Social Spending and Economic Growth Since the Eighteenth Century.* 2 vols. New York: Cambridge University Press, 2004.

Locke, John. *The Treatises of Government.* New York: Cambridge University Press, 1960.

Lomasky, Loren E. "Classical Liberalism and Civil Society." In *Alternative Conceptions of Civil Society,* ed. Simone Chambers and Will Kymlicka. Princeton, N.J.: Princeton University Press, 2002.

Lowy, Michael. "Twelve Theses on the Crisis of 'Really Existing Socialism.'" *Monthly Review* 43 (May 1991): 33–40.

Lucas, Robert E., Jr. "The Industrial Revolution: Past and Future." *The Region, 2003 Annual Report Edition.* Federal Reserve Bank of Minneapolis (May 2004): 5–20.

Mandeville, Bernard. "The Grumbling Hive: or Knaves Turn's Honest" (1705). *The Fable of the Bees,* ed. F. B. Kaye. Oxford: Clarendon Press, 1924.

Mansbridge, Jane J., ed. *Beyond Self-Interest.* Chicago: University of Chicago Press, 1990.

Margalit, Avishai. *The Decent Society.* Cambridge, Mass.: Harvard University Press, 1995.

Margolis, Howard. *Selfishness, Altruism and Rationality: A Theory of Social Choice.* New York: Cambridge University Press, 1982.

Marx, Karl. *Capital: A Critique of Political Economy.* New York: International Publishers, 1867.

———. *The German Ideology.* New York: International Publishers, 1970.

Mill, John Stuart. *A System of Logic.* London: Longmans, Green, Reader and Dyer, 1875.

———. *Essays on Some Unsettled Questions of Political Economy.* London: Longmans, Green, Reader and Dyer, 1884.

Mises, Ludwig von. "Economic Calculation in the Socialist Commonwealth." In *Collectivist Economic Planning: Critical Studies on the Possibilities of Socialism,* ed. Friedrich Hayek. London: Routledge, 1935.

Moffitt, Robert. "Incentive Effects of the U.S. Welfare System: A Review." *Journal of Economic Literature* 30 (March 1992): 1–61.

Munasinghe, Mohan. "Is Environmental Degradation an Inevitable Consequence of Economic Growth: Tunneling Through the Environmental Kuznets Curve." *Ecological Economics* 29 (1999): 89–109.

Munasinghe, Mohan, Osvaldo Sunkel, and Carlos de Miguel, eds. *The Sustainability of Long-term Growth.* London: Edward Elgar, 2001.

Murray, Charles. *In Pursuit of Happiness and Good Government.* San Francisco: Institute for Contemporary Studies, 1994.

Myers, Milton L. *The Soul of Modern Economic Man: Ideas of Self-Interest, Thomas Hobbes to Adam Smith.* Chicago: University of Chicago Press, 1983.

Myrdal, Gunnar. *The Political Element in the Development of Economic Theory.* Cambridge, Mass.: Harvard University Press, 1961.

Nordhaus, William, and James Tobin. "Is Growth Obsolete?" In *Economic Growth,* National Bureau of Economic Research, General Series 96E. New York: Columbia University Press, 1972.

Novak, Michael. *The Catholic Ethic and the Spirit of Capitalism.* New York: The Free Press, 1993.

———. *The Spirit of Democratic Capitalism.* New York: Simon & Schuster, 1982.

Nozick, Robert. *Anarchy, State and Utopia.* Oxford: Blackwell, 1974.

Okin, Susan Moller. *Justice, Gender and the Family.* New York: Basic Books, 1989.

Oliver, Henry M., Jr. "Attitudes Toward Market and Political Self-Interest." *Ethics* 65 (April 1955): 171–80.

Ostrom, Elinor, Laurie Gardner, and James Walker. *Rules, Games and Common-Pool Resources.* Ann Arbor: University of Michigan Press, 1994.

Paine, Lynn Sharpe. "Managing for Organizational Integrity." *Harvard Business Review* 72 (April–May 1994): 106–17.

Phillips, Anne. "Feminism and Civil Society." In *Alternative Conceptions of Civil Society,* ed. Simone Chambers and Will Kymlicka. Princeton, N.J.: Princeton University Press, 2002.

Polanyi, Karl. *The Great Transformation.* New York: Farrar & Rinehart, Inc., 1944.

Popper, Karl. *Conjectures and Refutations: The Growth of Scientific Knowledge.* London: Routledge, 1963.

Prasch, Robert E., and Falguni Sheth. "The Economics and Ethics of Minimum Wage Legislation." *Review of Social Economy* 57 (December 1999): 465–87.

Rand, Ayn. *Atlas Shrugged.* New York: Penguin Books, 1957.

Rawls, John. *A Theory of Justice.* Cambridge, Mass.: Harvard University Press, 1971.

Robertson, Ross M. *History of the American Economy.* 3d ed. New York: Harcourt Brace Jovanovich, 1973.

Robbins, Lionel. *The Nature and Significance of Economic Science.* London: Macmillan, 1932.

Roethlisberger, F. J., and William J. Dickson. *Management and the Worker.* Cambridge, Mass.: Harvard University Press, 1939.

Rowthorn, Robert. *Ethics and Economics: An Economist's View.* London: Routledge, 1996.

Ryerson, T. B., M. Trainer, J. S. Holloway, et al. "Observation of Ozone Formation in Power Plant Plumes and Implications for Ozone Control Strategies." *Science* 292 (April 2001): 719–23.

Sanborn, Henry, N. *What, How, for Whom: The Decisions of Economic Organization.* Baltimore: Cotter-Barnard Company, 1972.

Sandal, Michael J. *Democracy's Discontent: America in Search of a Public Philosophy.* Cambridge, Mass.: Harvard University Press, 1996.

Santelli, Anthony, Jr., Jeffrey Sikkenga, Robert A. Sirico, Steven Yates, and Gloria Zúñiga. *The Free Person and the Free Economy.* Lanham, Md.: Lexington Books, 2002.

Schneider, John R. *The Good of Affluence: Seeking God in a Culture of Wealth.* Grand Rapids, Mich.: William B. Eerdmans, 2002.

Schultz, Walter J. *The Moral Conditions of Economic Efficiency.* Cambridge: Cambridge University Press, 2001.

Schumpeter, Joseph A. *History of Economic Analysis.* New York: Oxford University Press, 1954.

———. "The Instability of Capitalism." *Economic Journal* 38 (1928): 361–86.

———. *Capitalism, Socialism and Democracy.* New York: Harper, 1942.

Seligman, Adam B. "Trust and Civil Society." In *Trust and Civil Society*, ed. Fran Tonkiss and Andrew Passey. New York: St. Martin's Press, 1996.

———. "Civil Society as Idea and Ideal." In *Alternative Conceptions of Civil Society*, ed. Simone Chambers and Will Kymlicka. Princeton, N.J.: Princeton University Press, 2000.

Sen, Amartya K. "Rational Fools: A Critique of the Behavioral Foundations of Economic Theory." In *Scientific Models and Men*, ed. H. Harris. London: Oxford University Press, 1978. Reprinted in Jane J. Mansbridge, ed., *Beyond Self-Interest.* Chicago: University of Chicago Press, 1990.

Serageldin, Ismail, and Christiaan Grootaert. *Defining Social Capital: An Integrating View.* Washington, D.C.: World Bank, 1997.

———. *Monitoring Environmental Progress – A Report on Work in Progress.* Washington, D.C.: World Bank, 1995.

Serra, Renata. "The Causes of Environmental Degradation: Population, Scarcity and Growth." In *The Economics of Environmental Degradation: Tragedy of the Commons*, ed. Timothy Swanson. Cheltenham: Edward Elgar, 1996.

Shklar, Judith N. *The Faces of Injustice.* New Haven, Conn.: Yale University Press, 1990.

Smith, Adam. *The Wealth of Nations* (1776). New York: Modern Library Edition, 1990.

Strassman, Diana. "Feminist Economics." In *The Elgar Companion to Feminist Economics*, ed. Janice Peterson and Margaret Lewis. Cheltenham: Edward Elgar, 1999.

Sturm, Douglas. "Economic Justice and the Common-wealth of People." In *Religion and Economic Ethics*. Vol. 1, ed. Joseph F. Gower. Lanham, Md.: University Press of America, 1990.

Sunstein, Cass R. *Free Markets and Social Justice.* New York: Oxford University Press, 1997.

Swanson, Timothy, ed. *The Economics of Environmental Degradation: Tragedy of the Commons.* Cheltenham: Edward Elgar, 1996.

Thompson, Grahame, Jennifer Frances, Rosalind Levacic, and Jeremy Mitchell. *Markets, Hierarchies, and Networks.* London: Sage Publications, 1991.

Thurow, Lester C. *The Zero-sum Society: Distribution and the Possibilities for Economic Change.* New York: Basic Books, 1980.

Tocqueville, Alexis de. *Democracy in America* (1835). New York: Penguin Classics, 2001.

Tomer, John F. *Organizational Capital: The Path to Higher Productivity and Well-being.* New York: Praeger Publishing Co., 1987.

Tonkiss, Fran, ed. *Trust and Civil Society.* New York: St. Martin's Press, 2000.

Unger, Roberto Mangabeira. *Democracy Realized: The Progressive Alternative.* London and New York: Verso, 1998.

U.S. Bureau of the Census, *Current Population Report*, http://www.census.gov/prod/1/pop/p60–191.pdf, (Washington, D.C.: U.S. Bureau of the Census, 1996).

U.S. Merit Systems Protection Board, "Sexual Harassment in the Federal Workplace: Trends, Progress, Continuing Challenges." *A Report to the President and the Congress of the United States.* Washington, D.C., 1997.

Vanberg, Viktor. *Rules and Choice in Economics.* London: Routledge, 1994.

Veblen, Thorstein. *The Theory of Business Enterprise* (1902). New York: New American Library, 1932.

Von Nell-Breuning, Oswald, S. J. *Reorganization of Social Economy.* Chicago, Milwaukee, and New York: The Bruce Publishing Company, 1936.

Walzer, Michael. *Toward a Global Civil Society.* Oxford and Providence, R.I.: Berghahn Books, 1995.

———. *Spheres of Justice: A Defense of Pluralism and Equality.* New York: Basic Books, 1983.

———. "Equality and Civil Society." In *Alternative Conceptions of Civil Society,* ed. Simone Chambers and Will Kymlicka. Princeton, N.J.: Princeton University Press, 2002.

Weber, Max. *The Protestant Ethic and the Spirit of Capitalism* (1905). Chicago: Fitzroy, Dearborn Publishers, 2001.

Weinberg, Daniel H. "A Brief Look at Postwar U.S. Income Inequality," Current Population Report, http://www.census.gov/prod/1/pop/p60–191.pdf (Washington, D.C.: U.S. Bureau of the Census, 1996).

White, James Boyd. "Economics and Law: Two Cultures in Tension." *Tennessee Law Review* 54 (Fall 1986): 161–202.

Williamson, Samuel H. "An Index of the Wage of Unskilled Labor from 1774 to the Present." *Economic History Services* (March 17, 2003): URL: http://www.eh.net/hmit/databases/unskilled wage/.

Women's International Network News. "Trafficking of Burmese Women and Girls into Brothels in Thailand." *Women's International Network News* 20 (Spring 1994): 34.

Woodstock Theological Center, Ethics and Public Policy Program. *The Ethics of Lobbying: Organized Interest, Political Power, and the Common Good.* Washington, D.C.: Georgetown University Press, 2002.

World Bank. *Monitoring Environmental Progress – A Report on Work in Progress.* Washington, D.C.: World Bank, 1995.

Wuthnow, Robert. *Christianity and Civil Society: The Contemporary Debate.* Valley Forge, Pa.: Trinity Press International, 1996.

Yeager, Leland B. "Ethics as Social Science." *Atlantic Economic Journal* 24 (March 1996): 1–18.

Zamagni, Stefano. "Hacia una Economía Civil." *Criterio* 70 (October 1997): 24–8.

Index

advertising, 60, 69
Alford, Helen J., 2
allocation, 79–83, 91, 94, 137
Altmeyer, Arthur J., 74
anarchism, 128, 131
Anasazi, 84
Andolson, Barbara Hilkert, 78
antitrust laws, 81
Aquinas, Thomas, 39, 70, 135, 136,
    155
Aristotle, 70, 159
Arrow, Kenneth J., 137
asian tigers, 2
Association of the Study of Peak Oil
    and Gas, 65

Bellamy, Edward, 32, 54–55,
    155
Bennett, William J., 4, 159
Berger, Peter L., 38, 143, 155
bigotry, 48
Blank, Rebecca M., 52, 69, 88, 96,
    156
Breitenbach, Hans, 121
Brennan, Geoffrey, 16
Buchanan, James M., 15, 16, 17, 18,
    20, 21, 22, 23, 24, 30, 116, 117,
    124, 127, 133, 156
bureaucracy, 89

Caldwell, Bruce J., 31
campaign financing, 120, 151
capitalism, 11, 13, 28, 31, 34, 35, 40,
    44, 54, 55, 58, 59, 61, 62, 64, 65,
    69, 72, 94, 96, 106, 121, 123
cartels, 81
Chambers, Simone, 142
child labor, 112
civil rights, 69
civil society, 139–144
Clark, John Bates, 45, 46, 156
Cobb, John B., 63, 86
co-determination, 138
common good, 16, 19, 20, 32, 43, 45,
    139
common pool resources, 85
communitarianism, 129, 141
Condorcet, 50
consequentialism, 26, 71
consumer sovereignty, 79
consumerism, 51, 68–69
corporate culture, 137
corporations, 2, 59, 71, 114, 138,
    149
corruption, 52, 90
Cropsey, Joseph, 16, 40, 157
culture, 4, 24, 51, 68–70, 71–73, 88
culture wars, 5, 125
Curran, Charles E., 72